"When we lost our baby unexpectedly, silence filled my soul. By the grace of God, Abbey does the impossible in *Held* by putting words to our pain in miscarriage while offering the hope of the gospel. She guides the broken hearted woman into the endless grace of God."

**Gretchen Saffles, Founder, Well-Watered Women**

"It was no coincidence that Abbey was writing *Held* when we lost our second baby. The portions of it that she shared with me were a balm to my aching heart. This is a Word-saturated book, tenderly written by a woman who loves Jesus, trusts him, and wants to see many hurting moms do the same. I highly recommend it to you."

**Kristen Wetherell, Author, *Fight Your Fears* and *Hope When It Hurts***

"I will always keep a copy of *Held* on my bookshelf to share with mothers enduring the pain of miscarriage. I am abundantly grateful to have a resource that reassures grieving mothers of God's presence, nearness, and purpose, even in the hardest days."

**Hunter Beless, Founder, The Journeywomen Podcast**

"Abbey Wedgeworth wants her book to be a companion in a season of loss. That is what we need, and that is what she has written. As she gently works through the difficult loss of an unborn child, she introduces you to a compassionate God who knows how to walk with you as your ultimate Companion. If you are experiencing or have experienced any kind of loss, you will find comfort in this book."

**Dr. Timothy Lane, Founder, The Institute for Pastoral Care**

"The pain of miscarriage is often hidden from view. It can be hard to articulate the many complex emotions that follow. Those struggling need hope! Written by people who have been there, *Held* offers just that. It's real, it's raw, but, most importantly, it helps individuals relate to Jesus and, even in the toughest of times, become more like him."

**Helen Thorne, Director of Training and Resources,
Biblical Counselling UK**

"With the compassion of one who's been there, Abbey Wedgeworth provides the space to grieve as well as the truth that will help heal. Through biblical teaching, vulnerable transparency, and honest reflection, *Held* will ultimately point you to the One who holds us all."

**Courtney Doctor, Coordinator of Women's Initiatives, The Gospel
Coalition; Visiting Instructor, Covenant Theological Seminary**

"Insightful, Scripture-saturated, honest, helpful, this book will offer warm companionship to those who have faced the devastation of miscarriage."

**Nancy Guthrie, Author, *Hearing Jesus Speak Into Your Sorrow***

"I found myself nodding through each chapter and saying, "I didn't know that other women felt this way too!" Abbey Wedgeworth feels like the best kind of friend to journey with. This wonderful devotional will be an invaluable companion for anyone who wants to find hope and help as they process their grief."

**Vaneetha Rendall Risner, Author, *The Scars That Have Shaped Me***

"Abbey Wedgeworth writes with the compassion and grace of someone who's walked this uniquely painful road, journeying along-side the reader to acknowledge the isolating and often unspoken struggles of miscarriage, while gently pointing her to the riches of Christ's comfort, hope, and truth. If you've walked through a miscarriage or know someone who has, this book will meet you where you are and offer you what you most need."

**Sarah Walton, Author, *Hope When It Hurts* and**
***Together Through the Storms***

"As a counselor I often look for resources to help my clients walk through various kinds of suffering. For anyone experiencing miscarriage, *Held* will be my go-to resource! Abbey and a collection of other voices speak so well to every angle of this painful experience. They hold the reader's hand, walking them back to the Lord over and over."

**Hope Blanton LMSW, Co-author, *At His Feet Bible Studies***

"*Held* is a Word-saturated and hope-filled companion that casts the eye vertically to God and then horizontally to those who have suffered a miscarriage. It offers life-giving truths amid the life-taking impact of the fall to those suffering, as well as those who seek to come alongside them with compassionate empathy."

**Karen Hodge, Coordinator of Women's Ministries, Presbyterian**
**Church in America; Author, *Transformed: Life-taker to Life-giver***

"*Held* sheds light and hope on a subject that is often dealt with in the lonely and quiet places. This is a resource I will use time and time again to offer comfort to the many families who deal with the grief of loss and need to be pointed back to the hope found in Jesus."

**Jerrad Lopes, Author, *Dad Tired & Loving It*; Founder, DadTired**

# Held

thegoodbook
COMPANY

Held
© Abbey Wedgeworth, 2020.
Reprinted 2020.

Published by:
The Good Book Company

thegoodbook.com | thegoodbook.co.uk
thegoodbook.com.au | thegoodbook.co.nz | thegoodbook.co.in

The image on page 77 is used by permission of Arab World Ministries
(www.awm-pioneers.org).

ISBN: 9781784984779 | Printed in Turkey

Design by André Parker

# CONTENTS

*To each woman who served as a reader for this resource in the days that followed the loss of life in her own womb.*

*This book is dedicated to you and to the lives you carried—fearfully, wonderfully, and purposefully made.*

# Introduction

Were we together in person, and were you to entrust me with the news of the passing of your little one, I would probably just sit with you. I might ask questions and listen, or I might bring you a meal, fold your laundry, or clean your kitchen while you regain your strength. In my own experience of losing life in the womb, I found that these gestures were often more powerful than words.

It feels strange to offer you a book filled with words when I know both the pain they can cause and the comfort of service in silence. But this book is designed to serve you—to be a companion in the wake of your loss: one that sits with you in silence and gently asks some of the questions I would were we together, giving you space to process.

These pages are not filled with feel-good sentiments or fluffy ideas. Their contents are based on something you can cling to—something steady and unchanging: the character and word of God. This book will not shy away from the questions you have, the raw emotions you may be feeling, or the temptations you face in your grief.

But it will offer something concrete and eternal to hold onto at a time when perhaps it feels as if everything is slipping through your fingers.

Each of these 31 devotions hangs on a verse or verses from Psalm 139. At the end of each devotion, you will find a collection of Bible verses to *read*, a question or two to help you *reflect* and process what you've read, and a prompt or printed prayer with which you can *respond*. Use these, and the book as a whole, at your own pace, whenever you're ready.

You will find pieces of my own story within these pages. But just as every miscarried child is unique, so is each experience of miscarriage and each way of responding to it. For this reason, I have included testimonies from other voices who have known the sorrow of miscarriage and the goodness of God within it. I have found companionship and comfort in these stories. I hope you will too.

One of the women I asked to read and review these chapters as I wrote them was the mother of a stillborn baby girl. Though this book was written with early pregnancy loss in mind, she felt confident that it may also benefit mothers who have lost a baby they carried well beyond the first trimester. If this is you, I hold it out to you as well. Though I cannot fully understand your loss or trauma, I do know that the same God who walked with me and that reader now walks with you.

Whatever your story of loss, and however you feel about it as you read these lines, I am praying for you. I pray that as you journey through this book, you would come to trust God more fully and treasure his word more deeply. I pray that you would become more aware of and more confident in his comfort and care, believing that even here, in the sorrow of miscarriage, you are held.

> *... even there your hand shall lead me, and your right hand shall hold me.* —Psalm 139 v 10

*Abbey Wedgeworth*

abbeywedgeworth

abbeywedgeworth.com

# The Character of God

*"I've never been this close to death. It's literally inside of me. Where life should be."*

I journaled these words a few days after we learned that our baby's heart had stopped beating in my womb. They called it a "missed miscarriage." At our first appointment, we had rejoiced to hear the beating heart of a much-loved child; four weeks later there was only silence and a lifeless form that hadn't grown at all. I couldn't wrap my mind around it. The lifeless baby within my womb was still so small, but the burden of the questions that accompanied that child's passing weighed me down and made it difficult to breathe at times.

Apart from dying ourselves, I'm not sure it's possible to experience death more personally than to have it occur within us. When the experience of death is that personal, trite religious phrases and sympathy-card expressions become more difficult to utter and even more difficult to accept. The days and months that followed our miscarriage held moment after moment that forced me to confront what I truly believed. *Where is God? How could he allow this to happen? If this could happen, what other kinds of suffering may be lurking around the corner for me? Does he see? Does he care? Is he punishing me? Is he trying to teach me a lesson? What did I do to deserve this?*

Psalm 139 is likely a familiar psalm for you. You've probably encountered its fourteenth verse on a hand-lettered coffee mug or sweatshirt, in some social-media post, or in some talk about loving your body. But if we read Psalm 139 in its entirety, we discover that this is not a psalm about us at all. It's a psalm about God. Within it we see that he is all-knowing, outside time, ever-present, incomprehensible, and all-powerful.

But observing all these attributes of God offers us no comfort at all in a time like this if we fail to truly understand his nature. Suffering tempts us to believe that God is absent, cruel, manipulative, or unconcerned, but the Bible offers us the truth. Through his word, God gives us more than an opportunity to learn *about* him. Because he is a God who wants to be known, because he is a God who wants a relationship with his people, he reveals himself to us. He declares that he is loving and good. He invites us to rest in that love and goodness, and to see that they underpin all of his attributes and actions.

Right now, at the outset of our journey together, in the wake of the tragic loss of the life you carried in your womb, I want to be honest about the choice that I think is before you. You can choose to allow your circumstances to shape your understanding of who God is, or you can allow what the Bible says about who God is to inform how you respond to your grief. What you believe about God will shape your experience of walking through this trial. It will have everything to do with the way that you heal and move forward.

This choice is not an easy one. And it will confront you over and over as you walk through these days. But it is a choice that is made much easier as we consider the ultimate display of God's loving nature: this God gave up his own Son for us. When we remember this act of love and faithfulness, these other characteristics described in Psalm 139 become a comfort. At the cross, God too experienced the loss of a child. This was not only to redeem a world he loved, but also, if you are trusting him, specifically to bring comfort, assurance, protection, and purpose in the very sorrow that you are currently experiencing.

The experience of miscarriage is tragic and traumatic. If you are anything like me, in your quest for truth and footing, you will be tempted to turn inward, allowing your feelings to shape your thinking. You will be tempted to focus outward, basing your understanding on your circumstances. But I want to encourage you instead, friend, to look upward. Look upward and be encouraged that the God who is all-knowing is not only aware of every detail of what you are experiencing, thinking, and feeling, but is also deeply concerned.

This God who knows you intimately is able to care for you perfectly. The God who is always present is with you, even *now*. He will never leave you (nor can you escape him!). The God who is incomprehensible offers relief to your tired and finite mind, sharing with you the knowledge you need and beckoning you to trust him with what you cannot bear. And this all-powerful God is sovereign even in this horrible experience, working it out for your good and his glory, just as he has always done.

You can trust him.

**READ:** Psalm 139; Psalm 34; Romans 8 v 26-32

**REFLECT:** How has this experience revealed or tested what you believe about God's character?

What do the verses above reveal about who God is? Which aspect is most comforting to you?

**RESPOND:** Confess the questions and doubts that you have out loud to God. Ask him to help you believe that he is who his word says he is.

**JOURNAL**

Ⓐ God protects us, hears us, delivers us, is close to the brokenhearted and saves those who are crushed in spirit.

Ⓑ I feel my emotions shaping what I think and that does not lead to truth. The bible alone is where truth can be found.

*O LORD, you have searched me*
*and known me!*
*You know when I sit down*
*and when I rise up;*
*you discern my thoughts from afar.*
*You search out my path*
*and my lying down*
*and are acquainted*
*with all my ways.*

*Even before a word is on my tongue,*
*behold, O LORD,*
*you know it altogether.*
*You hem me in, behind and before,*
*and lay your hand upon me.*
*Such knowledge is*
*too wonderful for me;*
*it is high; I cannot attain it.*

**PSALM 139 v 1-6**

# Nothing Is Hidden

Before I tucked the perfectly formed and fully intact sac and placenta into the tiny pink department-store jewelry box that would serve as our baby's tiny casket, I took a picture. As I put the lid on the box, I wondered why I'd snapped that photo. It seemed a strange thing to show someone, and I knew it would be equally strange to describe to anyone what I experienced in the hours before the "products of conception," as the doctors referred to them, left my body. It felt too private, too intimate, and perhaps too inappropriate to share.

The experience of miscarriage is a uniquely isolating grief because of the hidden nature of what is lost. The life you mourn never existed outside of you. Perhaps your eyes never beheld the form of your baby at all. Maybe you only saw a grainy image of your child on an ultrasound screen. Perhaps you held him or her when that tiny body left yours, or maybe he or she was carried away by a surgeon before you had the chance. Miscarried babies are seen by few eyes, and sometimes not even by those of their mothers.

Beyond a lingering, slightly rounded baby bump or an early ultrasound print-out, there's no tangible evidence that these babies were ever here. We've nothing to show for their lives. Our wombs are empty again, just as they were before. From the outside, no visible change seems to have taken place, and to anyone else, it's as if these babies never existed. No one but us felt their presence. Are we alone in missing them? Are we alone in remembering them?

This psalm makes it perfectly clear that the frame of your unborn child was not hidden from God. And just as he saw your baby's frame hidden within the darkness of your womb, he sees you now in the shadow of your experience with miscarriage.

In verses 1-6 of Psalm 139, the psalmist, David, sings of God's omniscience—his knowledge of everything. But he doesn't just recite this as a fact; he homes in on God's knowledge of us personally, particularly his full knowledge of our thoughts, our course, and our actions. From the time that you wake in the morning until the time that you lie down at night, and even as you sleep, David tells us, the eye of the Lord is upon you. Even as you struggle to articulate (or figure out) what you are thinking or feeling, God already knows it full well. As your lips fumble to form a prayer that you're not sure if it is appropriate to utter, he knows it completely.

He sees and knows *all* things.

As alone as you may have felt when you discovered the loss of your child, and however or wherever your baby left your body, you were not unseen by God in those moments. Nothing is hidden from God: not your baby, not your sorrow, not the untellable details of your trauma; not the events of your life, nor the course of your future.

And he is not merely a distant observer. In the book of Genesis we see this proclaimed by a woman named Hagar, who fled after being treated harshly by her childless mistress, Sarai, for becoming pregnant by her master, Abram, at Sarai's suggestion. In the wilderness, Hagar encountered an angel who told her that God had seen her affliction. The angel counseled her to return home, giving her courage and hope in the form of a promise about her future and that of her baby boy. She named this God "El Roi"—the God of seeing—saying, "Truly here I have seen him who looks after me" (Genesis 16 v 13).

The God who saw a hopeless and fearful Hagar in the desert, who showed up to offer her hope in the form of a promise, is the God who sees and shows up for you. This God is not simply a God who looks *upon* you, your trouble, or your thoughts, but—as Hagar proclaims—he is a God who looks *after* you. This God who is intimately acquainted with your ways, who searches and knows your heart and thoughts, is deeply involved in it all with his perfect care and his sovereign control.

The knowledge that God sees all things would bring terror to someone who had reason to fear his wrath and judgment; but for those who have peace with God through faith in Christ, who have been made daughters through the work of the Son, it is the best news possible. For us, his unlimited sight and perfect knowledge cannot be divorced from his infinite presence and care. Because he knows you intimately, he is able to care for you perfectly. And he does.

Perhaps calls and texts filled with sympathy and concern are pouring in from friends and family who love you; or perhaps few people are even aware of your loss. Either way, there are likely aspects of your grief, story, or self that feel invisible right now. Know that you are seen. As lonely, isolated, overlooked, or forgotten as you may feel, God—El Roi, the God of seeing—sees you. He knows you, he loves you, and he is actively caring for you even now.

**READ:** Genesis 16; Proverbs 15 v 3

**REFLECT:** What thoughts or details from your miscarriage have you not felt able to share? Have you felt "unseen"?

What does it feel like to acknowledge that God knows you and your situation even better than you do?

**RESPOND:** Talk aloud or use a pen and paper to tell God about the things that feel too private, inappropriate, or irrelevant to share with others. Offer him thanks for some specific ways you have experienced his care in the wake of loss.

## ✻ JOURNAL

Proverbs 15:3

"The eyes of the Lord are everywhere,
keeping watch on the wicked and
the good."

God knows me, He sees me, He
is always taking care of me.
These are helpful reminders of
truth when this suffering feels
so dark and heavy. Many in
my life have not experienced such
a loss, so it does feel like a
lonely road to walk.

God thank you for how you love
me and care for me. Please help
me to walk in your way. Please
give me peace in this grief.

# Man of Sorrows

*"I know exactly how you feel."*

I have yet to hear a story of these words being uttered to a bereaved mother in which they have not accomplished precisely the opposite of their intended effect.

Every experience of miscarriage is distinct. The details stand out so clearly in the mind of the mourning mother that the particulars of her loss can make her feel as if her pain is too unique for anyone to possibly understand what she is going through. As much as we hate feeling isolated, it's hard for us to imagine that anyone has ever hurt the way that we are now hurting. Words like these, even though they are motivated by the desire to comfort or relate, can make the details of our stories and perhaps even the lives of our babies seem insignificant by lumping them in with someone else's experience. Feeling dismissed, minimized, and more isolated, we inwardly reply, "You have no idea."

There will be some aspects of our experience with miscarriage which another woman can understand,

and others which she cannot. But Jesus understands us perfectly.

As we saw yesterday, this first portion of Psalm 139 declares God's omniscience: the fact that he knows everything. The psalmist highlights this attribute in verse 3 as he declares that God is acquainted with all of his ways. By referring to both his "path" (his outward actions) and his "lying down" (the things that happen in darkness, secrecy, or solitude), he shows us that God knows what is happening around us as well as within us—the visible and the invisible alike.

So, if it came from the mouth of God, the statement "I know exactly what you're going through" would be true. But hearing this expression of intended comfort, even from God the Father, might still cause us to feel alienated or belittled if we imagine him to be distant, disengaged, or unfeeling. We may be tempted to dismiss his words, just as we might dismiss marriage advice from a person who's never been married or tennis tips from a coach who's never played the sport.

But Isaiah 53 v 3 gives us the freedom to find comfort in God's words by offering our skeptical and wounded hearts a reason to trust them. Here we learn that God is not just "acquainted with all [our] ways," but that in Christ he became personally and intimately "acquainted with [our] grief." God knows your pain, not just theoretically by omniscience but concretely by his *experience* as a man.

Jesus made himself vulnerable by entering a womb in order to take on a human body that was every bit as physical as yours and mine, and every bit as susceptible to pain, hunger, fatigue, suffering, and even death. This incredible event—the Creator God becoming man—does away with any notion we may have that God is a distant, uncaring, unconcerned, or uninvolved deity. In the words of theology professor Kelly Kapic:

> *Even as our hearts are prone to question, filled with dread and doubt, let us take confidence that our God personally understands us, not hypothetically but concretely in Christ ... His ache and struggle give new meaning to our tears and suffering: God cares about our sin and distress so much that he enters into it himself.*
> —*Embodied Hope, pages 91-92*

Within a fully human body, Jesus felt the weakness of hunger and fatigue, the need to be alone, the warmth of tears streaming down his cheeks over the loss of a friend, the sharp sting of betrayal, the gut-wrenching feeling of being abandoned by those who were closest to him, and the dread and agony of anticipated pain and separation. He felt all this so intensely that his sweat was like drops of blood. The suffering of this "man of sorrows," as he is called in Isaiah 53 v 3, culminated at the end of his life, when he was physically beaten—his head punctured and scraped by a crown of thorns, his flesh torn by the cracking of whips on his back, his hands pierced through with nails to secure him to a cross, and his lungs filling with fluid as he suffocated. God—who is never hungry, who doesn't sleep, who cannot bleed—took on flesh in the person of Christ and fully experienced being human.

Jesus did not experience pregnancy loss. But because he is God, he does know exactly what you are going through; and because he lived as a man, he knows what it is to suffer.

But he did not come in human form *just* to be able to identify with us in our suffering. Jesus suffered so that he could redeem our suffering. He came to die so that we would never have to endure the greatest sorrow imaginable: eternal separation from God. "He was pierced for *our* transgressions. He was crushed for *our* iniquities ... with his wounds *we* are healed" (v 5, emphasis mine).

Jesus' death did not just save individuals from their sins, making them right with God; it accomplished a complete undoing of all of the horrible effects of human sin. Through his death and resurrection, Jesus overcame death itself.

This means that the suffering you are experiencing now can be redeemed. Christians experience suffering differently, because even in grief, we can know that we are children of God. We have access to God in prayer, the promise of his presence with us, the Holy Spirit to help and to comfort us, and the assurance that God will use our trials to build our character. Beyond these current comforts, the death and resurrection of Jesus also enable us to grieve with hope. We know that death will not have the final say and that we will share in his inheritance when he returns and we are raised with him.

On that day he will wipe every tear from our eyes—not because crying is an inappropriate response to suffering but because he will have taken away all need for grief.

Dear sister, God is intimately acquainted with every detail of what you are experiencing and feeling. Jesus was born in order to know your suffering, and died in order to redeem it.

Let the suffering of Jesus be the lens through which you see your own today. Cling to the Man of Sorrows, who suffered for your sake, and come to know more of him as you feel known by him in grief.

**READ:** Matthew 27 v 27-54; Revelation 21 v 4

**REFLECT:** What would someone know if they knew exactly how you feel right now?

How do you feel, knowing that Jesus went through physical, emotional, and spiritual suffering willingly—for you?

**RESPOND:** *Thou Knowest, Lord* (Jane L. Borthwick)

> *Thou knowest, not alone as God, all-knowing;*
> *As Man, our mortal weakness thou hast proved;*
> *On earth, with purest sympathies o'erflowing,*
> *O Savior, thou hast wept, and thou hast loved;*
> *And love and sorrow still to thee may come,*
> *And find a hiding-place, a rest, a home.*

 JOURNAL

# Praying Through Grief

I have never prayed more boldly than in the weeks leading up to our miscarriage. I have also never experienced a more definitive "no" to so many consecutive prayers. Our baby's limbs and organs did not form as I prayed for each of them specifically. The child's health was not granted. His or her life was not preserved. And then, though I pleaded, my body was not able to recognize what had happened and miscarry naturally.

Experiences like this can leave us confused. We "believe for" a miracle but don't get what we're begging for; we make ourselves vulnerable and end up feeling duped. Doubt, fear, and cynicism creep in and cause us to wonder: *Does God not hear me? Am I doing it wrong? Why pray at all if it doesn't make a difference?*

In verses 2 and 4 of Psalm 139, David helps us to lay the first of those questions to rest. Not only does God hear our prayers; he actually searches out our thoughts and knows the words on our tongues before we speak them. There is no point in even trying to keep our most honest emotions and desires from him. But as we consider this, our hearts may still be cynical: *Why bother praying if he already knows? And what's the point in baring my soul if he already knows what he's going to do anyway?*

Jesus' petition in the Garden of Gethsemane offers us a great deal of help as we grapple with these questions surrounding prayer in the wake of disappointment. On the night of his betrayal, he pleaded, "Abba, Father, all things are possible for you. Remove this cup from me. Yet not what I will, but what you will" (Mark 14 v 36). Luke 22 v 43-44 tells us that then "there appeared to him an angel from heaven, strengthening him. And being in agony he prayed more earnestly; and his sweat became like great drops of blood falling down to the ground."

The angel is God's response to Jesus' first request. He comes to strengthen Christ to do what he must. Matthew 26 v 42 tells us that the next time Jesus prays, he doesn't ask for the cup to be removed; rather he says, "My Father, if this cannot pass unless I drink it, your will be done." As the author and pastor John Piper points out, "He no longer prayed that the cup would pass, but for success in drinking it." ("The Greatest Prayer Ever Prayed," www.desiringgod.org)

Miscarriage finds us in that space of ungranted petitions, where cynicism tempts us to cease to pray altogether, whispering that God doesn't care or that praying doesn't make a difference. But in the example of our Savior we see that prayer is anything but pointless. When it becomes clear to Jesus that his prayer for a change in circumstances will not be granted, he prays all the more earnestly, "with loud cries and tears" (Hebrews 5 v 7), because he knows he needs the Father. His reaction to experiencing the "no" to his petition is to entrust himself and his circumstances to God. Jesus knows that God is perfectly able to change his circumstances but trusts that, even if he doesn't, his purposes are still perfectly loving and wise, and that he will provide the strength to endure.

In those lonely, intense, and agonizing moments, Jesus entrusted himself into the hands of his Father. And he had invited his followers to do the same, instructing them to begin their prayers the same way he would in Gethsemane: with the word "Father" (Luke 11 v 2). This address implies reverence and humility before authority, yes. But it also can be spoken with familiarity, warmth, and a sense of security.

Because of Jesus' perfect submission to his Father's will—his obedience to the point of death—as believers we can be confident that when we pray, we are not just heard as created beings but listened to as beloved children. The God who possesses all power, knowledge, and sufficiency loves us and is more on our side than anyone—even ourselves. Knowing this means we see his omniscience and omnipotence not as reasons not to pray but as motivators to pray. It is precisely the combination of his great power and his great love for us that should make us run to him when we are undone by the circumstances of our lives. Jesus won us that access by drinking the cup of God's wrath, so that when our own cup of suffering does not pass, we can draw near to the throne of God with confidence that we will receive mercy and grace in our time of need, just as Jesus was strengthened in the garden (Hebrews 4 v 16). Even when we don't know how to pray, the Spirit, who enables us to cry "Abba, Father," helps us in our weakness, interceding for us through wordless groans (Romans 8 v 15, 26).

Prayer will make a difference in your suffering, even if it doesn't make a difference in your circumstances, because it will undoubtedly make a difference in *you*. Day after day, as you bring your complaints, your laments, and your heartache to your Father, you will come nearer to his heart. Experiencing his listening ear and remembering his sovereign care and love for you will gradually uproot your cynicism. Little by little, you will move from hoping for a change of circumstances to placing your hope in the unchangeable God.

You can continue to pour out your heart, even in agony and disappointment, because of who you know God to be and because of who you are in Christ. God is your "Abba, Father." And you are a beloved child. From those two realities, take the assurance that you are heard, cared for, loved, accepted, cherished, and kept. Even if the circumstances of your life would incline you to believe otherwise, keep running to him with all of your questions, complaints, protests, laments, and desires for change. This all-knowing, all-powerful, completely good God loves you immeasurably and is able to provide all that you need.

**READ:** Romans 8 v 14-17; Matthew 6 v 7-13

**REFLECT:** What is your current attitude to prayer? How has your experience of miscarriage affected your prayer life?

In Matthew 6, how does beginning with the line "Our Father" influence the way you feel about praying "Your will be done"?

**RESPOND:** Spend some time pouring out your heart to God earnestly, asking specifically for the things that you need. This could be anything from help getting out of bed to an increase of faith, comfort, or peace; or the provision of someone to listen. Ask him to help you to trust him.

 **JOURNAL**

# John

My third pregnancy was always going to be risky. After prolonged sickness in my first pregnancy, I was utterly dismayed to find I couldn't walk six months into my second, finishing up in a wheelchair. I learned to walk again after many months, but the outcome of a third pregnancy was uncertain. Would I walk again if I had a third baby? How would I look after the two lovely boys I had already been given? Was it selfish to want a third?

When our youngest was two, I became pregnant again. I was daunted but hopeful.

Anxiety meant my prayers were fervent. I saw a physio straight away and spent hours doing the exercises I hoped would help me to walk. In the meantime, I was sicker than ever. It was not an easy time. But when we went as a family to my 12-week scan, my three-year-old saw his sibling safe inside his mother; he heard the heartbeat; he saw him move; my heart leaped.

My 20-week scan had been booked a couple of weeks early. This seemed to be an administrative error, but I was glad of any chance to see my little baby. The day before the scan I took my boys to a midwife appointment. They giggled at the midwife bending over me. She couldn't hear the heartbeat. "Don't worry," she reassured me. "It's not unusual at this stage. Your baby will just be hiding."

The following day I lay holding my husband's hand in the sonographer's room. "So, is the heart beating?" I asked lightheartedly. The answer came quietly; the sonographer was embarrassed as she spoke the few, small words which were terrible to hear. No. The heart was not beating. Our little one had died. I asked falteringly the only question I could think of—the question we had come to ask: could she tell, was it a boy or a girl?

It was a little boy. We knew exactly what we were going to call a third boy. His name was John.

I remember my husband gripping my hand very tightly when they told us our boy was dead, and I remember I just felt very cold, detached. It was only when I realised we would have to tell the news to our eldest, waiting excitedly at home, that I began to cry. I didn't stop crying for a very long time. Would the hospital just somehow "dispose" of this little life that I had carried—this little boy whose heart I had heard beating? They reassured me that I would be induced in a few days. An hour before, I had been expecting to leave the hospital elated by news of my baby. Now, as I left, I clutched leaflets advertising where I could bury him.

I carried him home inside me that day as I had carried him in, my large bump still proudly announcing a pregnancy to the world. My three-year-old couldn't understand the news. "I thought he was hiding, Mummy, like the lady said," he managed, in a whisper.

"He's not hiding, darling. His little heart has stopped beating. He has died. That's what God has decided, and we have to trust him."

"Why couldn't God decide that he could live?"

*I don't know, I don't know,* my heart cried.

The next day, John was still there inside me. I was a different woman now—a woman I didn't want to be, with a swollen stomach, swollen breasts, a dead baby. I didn't want to see anyone but my family. I carried John back to hospital with me a few days later—back to the birth unit where my other sons were born. I felt numb. It was unreal. I was induced, and he... emerged into the world. After the birth, some of the placenta was retained, and I kept bleeding. I found it hard to care.

It took another 24 hours before they could stop the bleeding. I was finally left to sleep. The blood which had left my body seemed to have carried all my hope and happiness with it. I had lost our last little boy. I had been able to hold him, to touch his delicate body. So small but so perfect. His little fingers with their little fingernails. That hand would never hold mine. I was discharged into a world that didn't understand. A few days later my milk came in.

I was very low for several months. I was struggling physically, but the spiritual and emotional battle was the hardest. I desperately searched Scripture for hope and the internet for answers. The first was wise; the second was not. I tried to be thankful. To thank God that we had held John. To thank God that he never had to know any suffering: that as "infants who never see the light" he was "at rest" (Job 3 v 11-16). To thank God for the promise that Christ will return and we can look forward to a perfect future with our Redeemer. But I felt desolate. I found it hard to relate to my husband. He did not feel the loss so keenly, nor did he see my body differently. I did. It seemed like a coffin to me.

Several years have passed. There have been no more children for us. Since the loss of John, I have learned to care deeply for those who suffer loss; I understand something of the horror of grief that I did not understand before. But the battle against bitterness and the fight for contentment and healing have been so much harder than I could ever have thought. I know the Lord is good and faithful; I know he does not ask his people to go through any more than they can bear. But carrying death within me has made my mind dwell more on death than it should. I need the Lord's help every day.

My greatest comfort is in the promise that, despite my ugly discontent and unbelief, despite my struggles with bitterness and envy, the Lord will not leave me or forsake me. One day I will be like him. How sweet that promise is!

# You Hem Me In

For a short season of my early married life, I ran a little online shop selling heirloom embroidered baby clothes. The pride of my work—and probably the reason that the business wasn't sustainable—was that I took the time to hem each little dress by hand. I would turn under a bit of fabric, press it, and then hide the tiny stitches under the fold. As a seamstress, I've always read this verse with that practice in mind: creating a boundary line for the end of the garment to give a nice finished look and to keep it from fraying.

The meaning of this word "hem" in the original Hebrew isn't quite as delicate. The Old Testament historical books use it in many cases to describe a city being "besieged" by armed forces in order to capture it or force it to surrender (for example, in Deuteronomy 20 v 12; 1 Samuel 23 v 8; 1 Kings 15 v 27). The author of this psalm, King David, was a soldier, and he is employing military language here to describe the experience of being surrounded as if by an enemy, conjuring up the feeling of being trapped. The language is uncomfortable because the experience is uncomfortable. We don't like to feel limited and powerless.

Miscarriage brings us face to face with our limits. Perhaps you've experienced your physical limitations as you suffer weakness from blood loss or the woozy effects of anesthesia. Maybe it's been presented in the pain of cramping as your uterus shrinks back to normal size. Have your fluctuating hormones induced night sweats, mood swings, or shakes? Perhaps you've been confronted with your mental limits in the inability to process, pay attention to, or understand all that is happening. Maybe your emotional limits have been put before you as grief takes you by surprise like a rogue wave. You can't seem to make yourself stop crying; or you can't work up the courage to allow yourself to start.

Miscarriage is an incredibly human experience. Miscarriage tells us we are limited.

But the psalmist, in one word, reveals the spiritual significance of these limits and helps us understand how we are to experience them: "You." He ascribes his limitations to God, crediting him with establishing and maintaining them. Just as God gives boundary lines to the ocean, telling it how far it may come (Job 38 v 11), and just as he holds the sun, moon, and stars in place (Psalm 8 v 3), so he sets limits on us by housing our souls within flesh. Frustrated as we may feel by it, our humanity is nothing to be ashamed of. When God formed Adam and Eve, before sin entered the world, he called what he had made—namely their bodies—good.

When Jesus took on flesh, he showed us the beautiful fruit that can come from being wrapped up in skin: humility.

> *Though he was in the form of God, [he] did not*
> *count equality with God a thing to be grasped,*
> *but emptied himself, by taking the form of a*
> *servant, being born in the likeness of men.*
> —*Philippians 2 v 6-7*

In the life he lived within the confines of human limitations, Jesus was hemmed in by hunger and thirst and bodily weakness. From that place, he demonstrated the beautiful sustaining power of living life in a posture of dependence on his limitless Father.

So often, rather than having the mind of Christ Jesus, as Paul encourages us to do in Philippians 2 v 5, we behave as if equality with God is in fact a thing to be grasped, by rejecting our own limitations. We try to manipulate our circumstances; we deny our hungry bodies food; we power through when we need to rest; we continue to lift when we know something is too heavy. But this refusal to exist as we were designed to exist leaves us more exhausted and stressed, not less.

It is a kindness of God to allow us to experience our human limitations. They enable us to appreciate his limitlessness, to know him more, and to live as we were created to live: in full dependence on our Creator. The humiliation we feel over our limitations can be transformed into beautiful gospel humility as we hear the call of our limitless God from the mouth of our incarnate Savior: "Come to me, all who labor and are heavy laden, and I will give you rest." The One through whom all things were made, and in whom all things hold together, describes himself as humble and invites us to learn from his example as we benefit from his humble and gentle service (Matthew 11 v 28-29; Colossians 1 v 16-17).

In this way, the frustrating experience of being hemmed in actually is rather like the hemline of a garment, because in deciding our limits and allowing us to experience them—in bringing us to the place where we feel frayed—God keeps us from unraveling by leading us to himself. And this is the beauty of being besieged and beset by God as the psalmist describes. Our surrender gives way to his sufficiency. Resignation gives way to rest.

God doesn't bring us to the end of ourselves because he is a bully who wants us to feel small, but because he is our gracious Father, who wants us to be at peace. Convinced of his strength and sustaining power, we can stop fighting and resenting our own humanity, and boast with the apostle Paul (2 Corinthians 12 v 10): "When I am weak, then I am strong."

**READ:** Isaiah 40 v 31; 2 Corinthians 12 v 9-10

**REFLECT:** How have you experienced the limitations of your humanity during your experience of miscarriage? What specifically has been frustrating for you?

What difference could the listed verses make to your experience of being "hemmed in" by your limitations?

**RESPOND:** *O Love, That Wilt Not Let Me Go*
(George Matheson)

*O Love, that wilt not let me go,*
*I rest my weary soul in thee;*
*I give thee back the life I owe,*
*That in thine ocean depths its flow*
*May richer, fuller be.*

 **JOURNAL**

# You Lay Your Hand upon Me

In the line "and lay your hand upon me," the word *lay* means "to put" or "to set." It is marked by gentleness. *Strong's Exhaustive Concordance* translates "your hand" as the hollow or flat of the palm. We are not gripped like prisoners and moved with the force of a tightly clenched fist, nor directed by backhanded blows. God's hand upon us is an open palm of gentle guidance. But gentle as it may be, it still directs us with power.

His hand purposefully guides us through difficulty rather than plucking us out of it. Just as he hems us in with physical limitations, the Lord keeps us in time and space with the gentle hand he lays upon us.

During my college years I worked as a camp counselor. We used to sing a song called "Going on a Bear Hunt" as we walked with children from one activity to another. In the song, we would come to various obstacles: long, wavy grass; a deep, cold river; thick, oozy mud; a swirling, whirling snowstorm. We'd act out wading or high stepping and make all the appropriate silly sounds of making our way through each obstacle to continue with the bear hunt. Each time the refrain would follow:

> *We can't go over it. We can't go under it.*
> *Oh no! We've got to go through it!*

Suffering is like this but not nearly as fun. We long for that hand to pluck us out of painful things and place us on the other side. We look for the way around suffering or over it, but the only path seems to be through it.

After such a long wait, I expected to be through it more quickly when our lifeless baby finally left my body. But our miscarriage was really just the beginning of a longer season of suffering. Apart from lingering sadness and weakness, the next few weeks and months held a debilitating back injury, an excruciating bout of shingles, and multiple painful biopsies because of a breast-cancer scare. Months later, I still felt as if I were walking through the valley of the shadow of the death of my baby. I longed to be over it: on the other side of grief and pain.

Yet true peace is found not on the other side of suffering but in the One who is by our side *through* it. Purpose, comfort, and rest are not discovered upon being through with suffering, but in being *brought* through it.

In Psalm 23 v 4, David declares the power of God's gentle hand upon him in trouble:

> *Even though I walk through the valley of the*
> *shadow of death, I will fear no evil, for you are*
> *with me; your rod and your staff, they comfort me.*

The rod was a club with nails hammered into it, designed to protect the sheep, and the staff was a walking stick with a crook, to guide them. These are what comfort the psalmist as he walks through the valley. God's hand is one of power, but also one of preservation, protection, and provision. He allows us to walk through dark and difficult places so that we might learn to love and trust his company and care. As we experience his presence, protection, provision, and power to preserve us within suffering, God invites us to remove our hope from anything we imagine to be on the other side of it and instead to place our hope in him.

It is a gift, this fact that God guides us in a way that makes us *walk* through the valley instead of rushing ahead—because that pace, moving slowly, forces us to be present. He gives us the opportunity to learn to trust him, step by step, as we wade through heartache.

And there is no other object more worthy of our hope. To allow us to place our hope in any other source, even in our circumstances, would be a cruelty. You may long to feel strong, capable, and unencumbered by sadness after your miscarriage—you may want to be out of this season and on to another—but the value of suffering is discovered in the midst of it as well as after it, for it is while we are walking through it that our frailty and weakness can convince us of our need for God's power and sufficiency. He hems us in and holds us there that we might know more of him personally and intimately.

In the final portion of Psalm 23, David stops walking

through trouble to pause and feast in the midst of it:

*You prepare a table for me in the presence of my enemies. You anoint my head with oil; my cup overflows. Surely goodness and mercy shall follow me all the days of my life, and I shall dwell in the house of the Lord forever.* —v 5-6

This feasting in the midst of suffering has been made possible for us, too. On the night he was betrayed, Jesus prepared a table for his disciples, inviting them to drink the cup of the new covenant. He then drank the cup of God's wrath so that we could say with the psalmist, even in the midst of suffering, "My cup overflows." We feast at the table that God prepares for us in the presence of the enemy that is death. So we can confidently say, "Surely goodness and mercy will follow me all of the days of my life. And I will dwell in the house of the Lord forever." Because of the finished work of Jesus, the ultimate "other side" of our suffering will be an eternity lived in the light of God's presence, with no more threat of sickness, sorrow, pain, or death.

But David declares that goodness and love will follow him "all of the days of [his] life"—not just upon his death. The promise of God's presence is a current reality for us, too, because God's Spirit is with us. The best news about your future in heaven is the best news about your life on earth too: God is with you.

May his promises for the future produce in us a greater hope than any other "other side" beyond this pain.

May his goodness, love, and comforting presence cause us to linger and feast, knowing his presence, in the season we are tempted to rush through.

**READ:** Psalm 23; Hebrews 13 v 6

**REFLECT:** What have you imagined to be on the other side of this experience?

In your mind, pull up a chair to the table God has set before you in the wake of your miscarriage. How have you observed his presence, protection, and provision?

**RESPOND:** Tell God how you long to be on the other side of grief and pain. Confess what you have been looking to and hoping for, rather than trusting in him. Praise and thank him for his comfort and care for you in the midst of this valley.

**JOURNAL**

# Searching for Answers

The shock and confusion that follow a tragic and unexpected loss can leave us feeling as if we've been duped or we've missed something. Attempting to catch up, our minds work in overdrive to piece things together, to connect the dots, to understand the hows and whys of what has happened.

Perhaps you've experienced some of these types of questions in the wake of the loss of your baby. *Was it something I ate? Did I exercise too heavily? Could my doubts about being ready for this baby have made my womb inhospitable? Was it a chromosomal abnormality? When did the baby pass away exactly?*

Perhaps your questions are more existential: *Why would God answer our prayers for a baby after years of infertility, only to take it away? Why would he give us a surprise pregnancy we didn't expect or ask for, let us love the baby, and then allow him or her to die? Why did this happen* again?

Our minds race anxiously, as if the path to peace and the way out of our pain is paved by our ability to make sense of the seemingly senseless.

*If I could just figure out what went wrong or the reason behind it, I could stop hurting so badly. If I could just figure out why and how this happened, I could rest.*

Although there is much we can learn through testing and ultrasounds, many answers in miscarriage are unavailable. In spite of what our minds may tempt us to believe, we cannot know or understand everything.

In Psalm 139 v 6, David acknowledges the limits of his own finite mind. He moves from simply declaring God's omniscience to confessing in humility that he, in contrast, does not know everything; even if he tried, he could not attain full understanding.

Asking questions in the face of loss is not sinful. We're in good company when we ask "Why?"

The book of Job contains a great deal of suffering, and a lot of "whys". At the end of the book, God responds to all of Job's questions, but not in the way we might expect. He doesn't offer Job specific answers to his questions about his suffering, but rather answers with himself: describing through rhetorical questions his sovereignty, his knowledge, his control, and his wisdom. Job responds to God with similar language to that of Psalm 139:

> *I know that you can do all things, and that no purpose of yours can be thwarted. 'Who is this that hides counsel without knowledge?' Therefore I have uttered what I did not understand, things too wonderful for me, which I did not know.*
>
> —*Job 42 v 2-3*

Job did what Eve would not. In the Garden of Eden, Eve reached for the knowledge held out to her by the serpent, believing it could offer her something more than the God who forbade it. The fruit of knowledge seemed sweeter to her than knowing God himself, and her pursuit of it led her away from him. Our tendency, too, is to believe that peace and satisfaction are found in *what* we can know rather than in simply and humbly placing our trust and finding rest in the One *who* knows. Job and David practiced the exact opposite of Eve's response to the serpent in the garden. In humility, they acknowledged God to be all-knowing and declared their own understanding to be limited. That is wisdom.

Our questions are not sinful in and of themselves. God welcomes our "whys." By bringing our questions to him, we acknowledge him to be the One who knows all things. But we err when we think he owes us an answer. We err when we think of him as a means to our intended end, rather than seeing that he is the end in and of himself.

At the foot of his throne, where we confess his knowledge to be greater than ours, we must not forget that he is a good God of perfect wisdom and love. Yes, he is incomprehensible, and so are his ways. But we can rest knowing that he has promised good to us, and all that he sends or allows operates to that end.

The truth is, knowing everything that led to the loss of your baby or all of the reasons behind your miscarriage wouldn't necessarily soften the ache or bring you rest or peace. But rest and peace are promised to us when we come to God with our questions and lay them at his feet in humility (Matthew 11 v 28-29; Isaiah 26 v 3).

In Deuteronomy 29 v 29, Moses encourages the perplexed Israelites toward humble obedience amid their wondering:

> *The secret things belong to the LORD our God, but the things that are revealed belong to us and to our children forever, that we may do all the words of this law.*

The eighteenth-century Bible commentator Matthew Henry wrote of this verse, "He has kept back nothing that is profitable for us, but only that of which it is good for us to be ignorant." We can trust that if God has not revealed it, it isn't something we need to know in order to grow or to grieve. We must labor to entrust the secret things to God, who is more on our side than we could ever be ourselves. He knows all things; he knows what is best for us.

Dear sister, even as your questions abound, cling to what you know—to what God has revealed: his Son, his character, his commands, and his ways. Let all of your "whys" lead you to the good "who." He doesn't promise to give us the answers, but he has given us himself: the God who is perfectly wise; the God who knows all things; the God who works for our good.

**READ:** Romans 11 v 33; 2 Samuel 22 v 31

**REFLECT:** What questions do you have surrounding the loss of your unborn baby? Take time to list them out. It's okay.

**RESPOND:** Talk to God about the things you wonder about and long to know. Ask him to give you faith in his perfect care and wisdom. Ask him to bring you rest and peace, even when you don't know all the answers.

 **JOURNAL**

ERIC SCHUMACHER

# Deceptive Voices[1]

Before it happened to us, miscarriage seemed to be a *woman's* experience, a *mother's* sorrow. I was not prepared for the internal struggles that confront a father and stunt his grieving.

Our first miscarriage occurred in September 2007, a year after the birth of our third child. The bleeding started the day after a home pregnancy test. Had my wife not taken the test, we might have thought her cycle had started late.

Close family members had just lost their baby in an ectopic pregnancy. Another family member miscarried several weeks further along. So we chose silence. We feared drawing attention away from their losses. How did the uncomplicated loss of an unexpected pregnancy compare to their painful and public suffering?

The temptation to compare myself with others reappeared with each miscarriage. I had not carried these children. I had not undergone a dilation and curettage (D&C).

---

[1] This testimony is a condensed and modified version of "Dads Hurt Too: A Father's Memoir of Miscarriage," www.risenmotherhood.com

I had not endured contractions, laboring to deliver a dead baby. *My wife* had. What was my experience compared to hers? Comparison pointed me to our living children too: "What right have you to mourn a child you never knew when you have these?"

When it came to the second miscarriage, another inner struggle arrived: shame. The doctor invited me to sit next to my wife during the D&C. I'd watched childbirth four times by then without flinching. Yet anxiety and nausea swept over me. I told her that I couldn't stay and exited to the waiting room.

I found a chair in an empty area. Shame took a seat next to me and started a conversation. "What kind of husband *abandons* his wife to suffer alone? What kind of wimp can't even hold his wife's hand while she goes through this?"

Late that fall we learned that another baby was on the way. We waited to tell our children until we heard the heartbeat. As the pregnancy progressed, so did our optimism. But at 16 weeks we learned that the baby had died. To avoid a D&C and in hopes of holding the baby, we chose induction and delivery.

At 4:40 p.m. on February 9, turned on her side, my wife felt a gush of fluid. Our 4.5-inch, 0.8-ounce baby was born. I saw the baby on the bed, wet with blood and amniotic fluid. Instinct told me to pick up my child and cradle its fragile body, so it would not lie there alone. But I didn't. I didn't know if I was allowed. Shame whispered, "What would the nurses say if they find you holding the baby?" So I just pressed the nurse-call button. As we waited for the nurse, the voice that discouraged me from holding the baby now chastised me for letting it lie. "What kind of a father lets his baby lie there?"

The nurses arrived, attended to my wife, and took the baby. The doctor, concerned about a stubborn placenta and excessive blood loss, rushed my wife to the operating room for a D&C. I waited alone, frightened and ashamed.

In the morning, we asked to see the baby. Shame told me this was foolish. "Now the nurse has to leave real, living babies to tend to you. She probably thinks you're an idiot."

That next Monday, we gathered around a little gravesite. I read Scripture and prayed before leaving our child for burial. Even making these arrangements with the funeral director brought shame. "He probably thinks this is ridiculous and can't wait to get back to real work."

In early 2015, having just moved to a new city, we discovered that, despite our decision to be finished having children, my wife was pregnant. We hit a wall of conflicting emotions. Pregnancy had grown increasingly destructive to her body. We hadn't wanted another child. Yet we treasure children. We knew we *should* want *this* child.

No sooner did our hearts warm to the reality of a new baby than the baby was gone, miscarried at five weeks. Waves of grief and emotion crashed over us. Grief over feeling grief at the news of the pregnancy. Grief over losing a baby that we now wanted. Relief at avoiding a painful and hard pregnancy. Guilt over feeling relieved. Shame had a field day.

This time shame brought a new friend to the party— loneliness. Few men know what to say or do to comfort a father mourning a miscarriage. Now we were in a new community—too new to have time-tested friendships. So, while my wife confided in a few, I stayed silent. How could I talk to my wife about *my* loss? How could I share this with other men? How could we mourn among people that never met the one who was missing? The loneliness multiplied.

It has been five years since our last miscarriage. I'd be lying if I said the struggles are gone. It is still hard to talk about. Even as I write this, I hear comparison, shame, and loneliness whispering. They tell me to be quiet and that a man has nothing to say about miscarriage. But I've been learning a few helpful things over twelve years of miscarriage.

I've learned to talk to Jesus. He knows all about death. He wept over it. He experienced it. He conquered it. He promises to free me from it. Who is better able to understand, to care, and to heal than him?

I've learned to talk back to those deceptive voices with the gospel. I tell comparison that I have a Father who notices and values the tiniest things of the world. "Fear not," Jesus assures me, "you are of more value than many sparrows" (Matthew 10 v 31). I tell shame that I have a Savior who is not ashamed of me. He bore the shame of my sin. He knows what it is like to suffer shame as a human. Therefore, he is not ashamed to call me brother (Hebrews 2 v 11). I tell loneliness that I am never alone or forsaken. Through the Holy Spirit, the Father and the Son have made their home within me (John 14 v 23, 25).

I've also learned to talk to others. Over the past decade, I've tried to be intentional in speaking of my weaknesses—the miscarriages, conflicts, depression, anxiety, failures, disappointment, and loss. The result is that men pull me aside, drop me an email, or call me and say in quiet tones, "We had a miscarriage. I don't know what to do."

So we talk. I listen to their grief. I offer what little wisdom and practical tips I can. I speak of Jesus, the Son who roared in the face of death and crushed its head. Then we ask the Father who hears and sees and knows to give us faith and hope and love.

It is with that hope that I offer my story—that grieving fathers and mothers might hear and find the freedom to speak, to grieve, to believe, and to heal.

# Marriage After Miscarriage

*"This was his child too, so why does he seem unaffected?"*

*"I'm the one whose body is ravaged, whose hormones are all over the place, who lost the blood, and whose womb is empty. He should be supporting me instead of needing me to support him!"*

*"I feel like he's rushing my grief, trying to get me to stop being sad instead of acknowledging that this actually is sad."*

*"Why hasn't he cried at all? He's making me feel like I'm crazy."*

*"He feels so distant and unavailable: why is he always leaving the house when I need him with me?"*

*"I thought grief was supposed to strengthen marriages."*

Perhaps one or more of these sentences echo your sentiments toward your husband since your miscarriage. For my husband, David, and me, the shock and grief of losing our baby took us out into uncharted waters. As we waded through them alongside each other, our sorrow over the loss was made worse by feelings of loneliness in a context in which we had only ever experienced support and unity. Have you experienced loneliness, pain, or frustration over the way that your spouse is grieving—or doesn't appear to be?

We've seen in this first portion of Psalm 139 that God is all-knowing and attentive, sovereign and unlimited, unbounded by time and space, perfectly wise, and gloriously impossible to fully understand. And these attributes are unique to him. It is greatly liberating for our marriages when we recognize that neither we nor our spouses are limitless in knowledge, attention, love, space, time, or wisdom. It is incredibly relieving to free our husbands from the burden we can subconsciously place upon *them* to be God. That is a burden they were never intended to bear.

Let's review the first six verses, thinking specifically about how they might bring clarity and freedom to marriage.

*O Lord, you have searched me and known me!*
*—v 1*

People can only draw conclusions about each other based on what they can see and hear, but the Lord sees and understands our hearts. When we remember that God alone has perfect knowledge of us, feeling misunderstood by a man doesn't seem so earth-shattering. God's concern for us is a comfort when it seems that our spouses are disengaged or uninterested.

*You know when I sit down and when I rise up;*
*you discern my thoughts from afar.        —v 2*

When we know that only God is able to discern our thoughts, we will recognize the importance of communicating with our spouses, rather than expecting them to be able to read our minds. We will be less offended when they touch us instead of perceiving that we'd rather be left alone, or when they leave the room rather than realizing that all we want is to talk. When we know that God alone is able to discern *their* thoughts as well, we will be able to stop presuming to understand the minds of our husbands and the motives behind their actions. We can move from assuming the worst and blaming them to patiently encouraging and affirming them.

> *You search out my path and my lying down*
> *and are acquainted with all my ways.* —v 3

Since the loss of the baby and the lingering effects of miscarriage take place within our bodies, our husbands can't identify with what we are experiencing physiologically, and in some cases they can't bear to watch the process or hear the details of the story. In those moments, when we feel loneliness or even abandonment, we can acknowledge their humanity and limited capacity to know and experience. We can rest in the knowledge that God sees, knows, and is with us where our spouses are unwilling or in that moment unable to go.

> *Even before a word is on my tongue,*
> *behold, O Lord, you know it altogether.* —v 4

Because we know God hears and listens intently to us, we don't have to be devastated when our spouses seem overwhelmed by our feelings or burdened by our words. Similarly, we can entrust our spouses to the One who hears, encouraging them to pray rather than pressuring them to process with us.

> *You hem me in, behind and before,*
> *and lay your hand upon me.*          —v 5

Even if our spouses feel far away and we can't quite figure out how to reconnect, we know that the presence of the Lord surrounds us. If we have confidence that God directs our paths and is sovereign over each of our experiences, we can accept the pace at which our husbands move forward—even if it is more quickly than us—without feeling bitterness, abandonment, or resentment toward them. Though we each experience this loss uniquely, as different people with different vantage points, we have the same sovereign hand of care and guidance upon us. You can look for the ways God is using your journey through grief to draw each of you closer to himself and bring you to a better understanding of how to love each other.

> *Such knowledge is too wonderful for me;*
> *it is high; I cannot attain it.*          —v 6

Neither you nor your spouse is all-knowing, all-powerful, or ever-present. Neither of you is perfect. But you have a perfect Savior in Christ Jesus. He lived the perfect life of faith that you never could, he died the death you deserved, and he lives seated at the right hand of the Father to help you. He gives you the grace you need, by the power of his Spirit, to be gracious with each other when you are disappointed in one another. As he shows you more of the lavish and unconditional kindness that has been poured out on you, you will be empowered to pour out that same kindness on your spouse.

An experience of loneliness or disappointment in marriage provides us with an opportunity to experience intimacy with God. Our own limitations, and the limitations of our spouses, point us to our need for a limitless God. When we see all the ways that God is different from us, when we see that he possesses what we long for, we are led to worship. And we stop looking elsewhere— to ourselves, or to the one lying next to us—to give us what we most need, and which only God can grant. Our marriages become safer, happier, and more secure when we stop expecting our spouses to be God, and look to God to do what only he can.

**READ:** Ephesians 4 v 32; 1 Corinthians 13 v 4-8

**REFLECT:** How has your husband's grief been similar to or different from your own? What do you long for from him right now? Take some time to consider his humanity. How might you offer love and support to him?

**RESPOND:** Confess any conviction you experienced while reading this devotion. Thank God for the forgiveness and grace you have received in Christ Jesus. Ask him to cause that forgiveness and grace to abound in your marriage.

 **JOURNAL**

*W*here shall I go from your Spirit?
     Or where shall I flee
from your presence?
If I ascend to heaven, you are there!
If I make my bed in Sheol,
you are there!
If I take the wings of the morning
and dwell in the uttermost parts
of the sea,
even there your hand shall lead me,
and your right hand shall hold me.
If I say, "Surely the darkness
shall cover me,
and the light about me be night,"
even the darkness is not dark to you;
the night is bright as the day,
for darkness is as light with you.

**PSALM 139 v 7-12**

# The God of All Comfort

My friend Melissa is an occupational therapist. She told me a story recently about a little boy she was working with. This boy, who has autism, became so overwhelmed by a task in therapy that he lost control of himself. She calmly urged him to take deep breaths; he nodded but couldn't stop gasping for air. And so she gently picked him up and carried him to a device that she refers to as "the swing."

In the center of this hammock-like contraption, the weight of the boy caused the fabric to cocoon around him, helping him become aware of his body in space, which is often difficult for children with autism. When overwhelmed, they sometimes lose their spatial awareness and begin to feel somewhat like an astronaut whose tether has broken, floating through outer space with nothing to hold onto. Being placed in the swing wakes children up from that nightmare, causing them to feel rooted, safe, and secure, like a cradled child in the arms of a father. So, as the fabric hugged the boy, he relaxed, regaining his composure and his breath.

The presence of God is like this.

In the midst of suffering, we may forget that God is always with us because his presence is not tangible—we can't just reach out and touch him. Or we feel as if he is too far away, so we flounder, like the boy, in what feels like empty space.

Regardless of whether we *feel* God is there, David assures us that his Spirit is indeed everywhere present. He declares that, from the skies to the ground, from the place where the sun rises to where it sets, and everywhere in between, God is with him. And the same is true for us.

On the cross, Jesus endured separation from God so that those who place their faith in him would never have to. He was forsaken so that we would *never* have to wonder either whether God is with us or whether he is for us. Jesus absorbed all God's anger, not only so that we could be with God but also so that we could enjoy his loving presence without fear of punishment or abandonment.

If you have trusted Christ for salvation, the presence of God is not just around you generally; he dwells within you personally through his Holy Spirit. And this is a source of supreme comfort. God's word assures us that through *Christ*, by the power of the Spirit, we share *abundantly* in God's comfort, in *every* affliction (2 Corinthians 1 v 3-5). The Holy Spirit reminds us of his presence with us, his posture toward us, and his promises to us in those times when sorrow or distress make us most prone to forget.

Any source of earthly comfort is temporary. We can

eat comfort food until we are sick, but eventually we will hunger again. We can watch Netflix until we fall asleep, but we will wake again. We can drink until we're numb, but we will be sober again. The only source of true and lasting comfort is God himself.

So how do we run to the swing of his embrace? How do we receive his comfort? God provides us with the means to enjoy his comforting presence through his word, through prayer, and through fellowship with one another.

We may not be able to physically feel him within or around us, but Scripture tethers our hearts to what is true when we feel ungrounded and uncertain. In it we hear him speak and are assured that he hears us when we cry out to him. As his truth informs our feelings and our hearts draw near to him in prayer, he comforts us with a peace that surpasses all understanding (Philippians 4 v 7)—an unshakable confidence that he is with us and for us, and that our souls are secure.

God also provides tangible expressions of his loving presence through people who share the fellowship of his Spirit. They remind us of who he is when we are over-whelmed and agitated, like my friend Melissa picking the boy up and placing him in the swing.

According to Melissa, using the swing can be fright-ening initially. Some kids panic, feeling pressed and restrained. But over time, even the most resistant chil-dren come to love it. Many parents purchase swings for their homes, making the hug of the device a regular part of their routine. Eventually, when these children start to feel agitated, they run to the swing, convinced of the soothing power of its embrace.

Some of us, like those children who initially feel smothered by the swing, feel that God is too close in suffering. We think of him as a tormentor. We question his goodness and his sovereignty as our pain and doubt cause us to wonder how he could possibly be both.

Job, in his suffering, laments that God won't leave him alone even long enough to let him swallow his own spit (Job 7 v 19). Perhaps David is thinking the same thing, adding to his analogy of being besieged by God when he asks, "Where shall I go from your Spirit? Or where shall I flee from your presence?" (Psalm 139 v 7).

If, like Job here, we think of God as the vindictive sender of our sorrow, we too may wonder how to escape him. But understanding what God is really like with his children moves us from imagining him as a harasser or heckler to seeing him as a source of solace and soothing—just as children come to love the swing's embrace.

If confusion and pain have caused you to want to say to God, like Job, *Just leave me alone,* remember this: the Spirit of God is not with you to torment you. He is a God of peace, and he has gone to great lengths to bring his peace to you through the death and resurrection of his Son. When we remember this, we will learn to love rather than lament his presence with us in our suffering. Let the weight of your sorrow and pain cause you to sink more deeply into the fabric of his embrace. Let yourself be comforted in the swing of his presence.

**READ:** Romans 8 v 35-39; John 14 v 27

**REFLECT:** Can you relate to the boy in the therapy session, feeling lost and overwhelmed? How would you describe your own emotional experience of grief?

Practically speaking, what might it look like for you today to run to and rest in the presence of the God of all comfort?

**RESPOND:** Tell God how you feel about his presence. Ask him to help you to trust in his character and nature. Tell him where you have turned for comfort. Then ask for his help to find comfort and rest in him—and him alone.

 **JOURNAL**

# A Very Present Help

*"Why is it so hard to just make chicken salad?"*

My sister answered the phone in tears. My call had caught her in the midst of trying to prepare a meal, with ingredients strewn all over the counter, struggling to assemble them. Her miscarriage, just days earlier, had come not even 18 months after the traumatic experience of her infant son having emergency open-heart surgery. Now, regulating her own heart rate and thoughts, and accomplishing even the simplest everyday tasks felt impossible.

Grief can have this effect. It consumes our energy, making our baseline overwhelmed so that picking up a spoon can feel like lifting a dumbbell. When we feel like that, how do we function? Where do we get the strength to get out of bed, to complete our tasks at work, to fold the mound of laundry that seems like a mountain, to care for a totally dependent toddler, or to prepare a meal when it feels like chaos has overtaken the kitchen and we don't even know where to start?

Or maybe for you grief has had the opposite effect: instead of feeling stuck to the starting blocks, you've thrown yourself into a full sprint. Rather than being overwhelmed, you're stuck in adrenaline-fueled overdrive, determined not to fall behind or depending on busyness to distract yourself from feelings you are afraid to feel. But no one can sprint forever. That burst of adrenaline will eventually wear off.

The presence of the Lord offers the strength that you need—whether that's the strength to begin or the strength to endure.

*God's presence is not only a source of comfort but also a source of help.* As Psalm 46 v 1 declares, "God is our refuge and strength, a very present help in trouble." God's present help is incredibly practical. We can find countless examples in Scripture of God's presence empowering his people. In the first quarter of the Bible alone, we see Joshua instructed by God to be strong in *his* mighty power, as he steps up to lead the people into the promised land; the Spirit of God rushing upon a weak Samson after failure and defeat, giving him strength to crush his captors by pushing down the pillars to which he is chained; and David, the shepherd boy, defeating Goliath the giant with only a sling and a stone. The presence of God empowers his people to accomplish the things he calls us to do, even and especially in our times of weakness.

The last two lines of this stanza of Psalm 139 encourage us that because God is ever present, his help is always available, even in the places where we feel alone and uncertain.

"Even there your hand shall lead me, and your right hand shall hold me" (v 10). Even there, he gives us his strength.

Life has no pause button. We want the demands of our lives to stop long enough to regain our footing, to grieve, to catch up; but the dishes keep appearing in the sink, the needs of our families must be met, bills still have to be paid, and work projects still have deadlines. The rest of the world keeps spinning as if nothing has happened, like a carousel we're too dizzy to ride but can't seem to get off. It is precisely in that place that the presence and promises of God become so sweet.

Through the changing of the seasons, the movement of the sun, the traveling of our bodies, and the fluctuations of our emotions, there is no place where he is not present to lead us and hold us. Acts 17 v 28 tells us that it is in God that we "live and move and have our being"; Jesus himself declares in John 15 v 5 that apart from him we can do *nothing*. We are always dependent on his strength and help for our very lives. Grief simply makes us more aware of our need.

So don't be discouraged if you feel shame over how weak you think miscarriage has revealed you to be. Your trials are not opportunities to discover how strong you are but rather for you to learn to depend on the strength of the Lord.

Maybe you feel paused on the inside while the rest of the world keeps going. Or maybe you're sprinting, but beginning to feel that you can't keep up this pace. If you're looking at the "hills" of the tasks before you, feeling powerless and overwhelmed, wondering, like the writer of Psalm 121, "From where does my help come?" you can repeat the response that the same psalm offers: "My help comes from the LORD, who made heaven and earth."

My dear sister, the Maker of heaven and earth surrounds you in your overwhelmed moments, enabling you to keep going and to live for him—by his very own power, which is made perfect in your weakness (2 Corinthians 12 v 9). Sometimes that provision comes in the form of the humility we need in order to ask for help from another person. The task that feels impossible for you today may be the good work he's calling another to do through service.

This is the message we need to hear in our moments of feeling powerless—not the worldly cry of *You can do it!* but rather the spiritual truth that *God can do it.* He is able to do far more than you could ever ask or imagine, according to the power that works within you (Ephesians 3 v 20).

That power is the Holy Spirit. If you have trusted Christ for salvation, you have within you the same Spirit who gave strength to Samson, victory to David, and courage to Joshua—the same Spirit who raised Jesus from the dead. The presence of God surrounds you. The Spirit of God is in you. He helps you and strengthens you to do the work before you.

The Lord is your help. Just do the next thing in his power and strength.

**READ:** Hebrews 13 v 20-21; Psalm 121 v 1-2

**REFLECT:** Would you describe your reaction to loss as overdrive, paralysis, or something different?

Make a list of the things that you are responsible for today, this week, and this month. Is anything unnecessary? Is there anything you can delegate? Separate the work you must do into bite-sized action items. Carry your list with you, asking for God's help with each "next thing" as you go.

**RESPOND:** *How Firm a Foundation* (George Keith)

> *Fear not, I am with thee, O be not dismayed,*
> *For I am thy God, and will still give thee aid;*
> *I'll strengthen thee, help thee,*
> *and cause thee to stand,*
> *Upheld by my righteous, omnipotent hand.*

 **JOURNAL**

**IRENE SUN**

# Carried and Cradled

Miscarriage. What an ugly word. Shortly after our baby died, I could not even come close to this word. Whenever I encountered it online or in books or in conversations, I looked away. I didn't believe I could ever talk about it "normally."

I was annoyed when the doctor attempted to console me. "This is very common," she explained. Well, my child's death is not common to me. I hesitated to answer when friends kindly asked, "How far along were you?" My baby was seven weeks old. Yes, it was early in the pregnancy. Yes, I have four other children. Their alive-ness, their presence only magnifies my one child who is absent.

I started bleeding on Monday morning, after Easter. We called the doctor right away. The doctor gave the order to be on bedrest and to come to the clinic on Wednesday. For three days I forced myself to lie motionless in bed. *Perhaps if I don't move, the bleeding will stop. Perhaps if I stay very still, I get to keep this child.* Even so, my body went into labor without my permission.

So, I hate the word "miscarriage." Unlike mis-understanding and mis-take, mis-carriage cannot be made right. And, it is entirely irreversible and out of my control. Even when every fiber of my being wanted to carry my baby, my body mis-carried. My body betrayed me.

On Sunday, we celebrated Christ's empty tomb. On Wednesday, we mourned my empty womb. The ultra-sound revealed a cavern of darkness. No sound. No heartbeat. Just black. Silence.

My womb, which had been a vessel of life for my other children, became a vessel of death. For three days my womb was a tomb for my unborn baby. We did not get to say hello. We did not get to say goodbye.

Lilias Trotter was a missionary in the deserts of Algeria. I kept a compilation of her journal entries and artwork at my bedside during our waiting. She painted in her journals. Intricate strokes and bold colors were juxtaposed with the faint blue lines of a common notebook. She painted in secret for the eyes of her God.

I held in my mind one particular image of a mother holding her child. She cradled her baby the way I wanted to cradle mine. I could almost smell the sweet baby's breath and feel the warmth of the mother's lap.

In the compilation of Lilias Trotter's works by Miriam Huffman Rockness, the painting of the mother and child was placed next to these words from Lilias's journal entry:

> *"Two glad Services are ours,*
> *Both the Master loves to bless:*

*First we serve with all our powers*
*Then with all our helplessness."*

*Those lines of Charles Fox have rung in my head*
*this last fortnight ... The world's salvation was*
*not wrought out by the three years in which He*
*went about doing good, but in the three hours of*
*darkness in which He hung, stripped and nailed,*
*in uttermost exhaustion of spirit, soul, and*
*body—till His heart broke.*

*So little wonder for us if the price of power is*
*weakness.*

*—A Blossom in the Desert, page 164*

Monday, Tuesday, Wednesday. I lay in bed helpless
and unhelpful. There is no weariness like the weariness
of being utterly useless. I had nothing to offer to the
Lord—nothing to give to my loved ones. I was like that
paralyzed friend who needed to be carried onto the roof

and lowered to Jesus' feet. For the first time, I understood the line in that timeless hymn: "Help of the helpless, O abide with me."

My beloved husband bore all the burdens of the household. He cared for me and for the older boys. He taught, fed, and bathed them while I stayed in bed. Friends came and covered our empty table with food. Their gifts bore whiffs of their souls—what they loved and their love for us. Roast chicken, warm soup, along with a bouquet of roses and daisies and lilies. There was also a box of creamy popsicles. We were not alone.

God said to Paul, "My grace is sufficient for you, for my power is made perfect in weakness" (2 Corinthians 12 v 9). I must confess, I am not quite like Paul. I found it difficult to rejoice in my frailty. I longed for the power of Christ; I longed for his joy and rest. I could not say, "When I am weak, then I am strong" (v 10). I was not strong, only weak.

My potter was making me. The only help I could give was to be still. I was a lump of clay. A lump of clay spun and whirled on my potter's wheel. A lump of clay pressed from every side, his firm hands breaking me. A lump of clay placed in the furnace, burning. A lump of clay, useless but wanted. A lump of clay, carried and cradled.

Will I thank him for his hands breaking and molding? Will I trust him when my head is spinning? Will I praise him in the furnace, burning?

He is here, in the breaking. He is here, in the whirling. He is here, in the furnace, burning. He makes no mistakes. He never misunderstands. He never leaves or forsakes—never miscarries.

Jesus Christ is our dwelling place. We are carried and cradled in his all-sufficient grace. "In him we live and move and have our being" (Acts 17 v 28). We belong to God because of Jesus' empty tomb.

We named our child Immanuel—"God with us." Little ones to him belong. We are weak, but he is strong. Yes, Jesus loves.

# The Language of Lament

*If I say, "Surely the darkness shall cover me,*
*and the light about me be night..."*

This fearful phrase was not just hypothetical for the writer of this psalm. David experienced his fair share of literal and spiritual darkness: running for his life, hiding in caves from his enemies, concealing his sin of adultery with murder, and grieving the loss of his sons to betrayal and death. When we are under the cover of this sort of darkness, it's easy to feel as if God has hidden his face from us.

It may feel as though the right and religious response to grief is to hold back your tears, extinguishing your out-of-line emotions with a firehose of biblical platitudes; but the psalms, which were intended to serve as a hymnbook for God's people, give you permission to say what it feels like to be in the dark. While this book of the Bible does contain hymns of joy filled with glad worship, over a third of the psalms are songs of lament. They are written from the sort of darkness to which David refers: from places of frustration, anguish, and sorrow.

In his word, God gives us songs to sing in the darkness—in our grief, guilt, or confusion. He offers us company in the writers of these songs and uses their words to give us language to voice our pain. He knew we would need them. He intends for us to sing them.

Psalm 13 is one such psalm. In it David—the same man who wrote the lines in Psalm 139 about how God is everywhere present—isn't so confident that God is with him. He's in turmoil and begins with honest questions that give us our first window into what healthy lament looks like.

*How long, O LORD? Will you forget me forever?*
*How long will you hide your face from me?*
                                    *—Psalm 13 v 1*

*Are you here? Are you doing what you said you would? Are you who you say you are?* Asking these sorts of questions and expressing our feelings honestly might feel prideful or irreverent, but lament is actually an act of humility and surrender: it brings our doubts and accusations, our complaints and outrage straight to the One we believe to be in control of everything. This is what makes lament so important. It is prayer without pretense. As we uncross our arms to throw up our hands in confusion and frustration, we leave them open in a posture of readiness and desperation. Lament leads our souls to an uncomfortable but honest place where they crave relief and are ready for answers. You can hear that desperation in Psalm 13 v 3: "Light up my eyes, lest I sleep the sleep of death!"

When we lament, we feel we are in utter darkness. But each complaint, each question, each cry of despair in the darkness lifts our eyes to see that God is the only source of light. That is the pattern of lament that we are offered in the psalms: questions give way to the truth that is so desperately needed.

Your feeling of being alone in the darkness can lead you to the reality that God is with you. Your fear that he has left you can move you to cling to the reality that he *never* will. Your doubts about his goodness and justice can cause you to acknowledge that he sets the standard for both. Your questions about how he could allow you to suffer if he really loves you can lead you to rest in the fixed reality of his love for you in Christ.

This is the shift that has happened to David by the time we get to verse 5 of Psalm 13:

> *But I have trusted in your steadfast love; my*
> *heart shall rejoice in your salvation. I will sing*
> *to the Lord, because he has dealt bountifully*
> *with me.*

When it feels like we have nothing left, we become beautifully aware that God is all we have. It becomes abundantly clear in the dark that his light is what we need the most.

As the Israelites traveled through the desert toward the land God had promised them, they followed a pillar of fire, which guided them forward in the night. In the darkness, they had only to look up and see the light of that fire to know he was with them. We are traveling too, saved from sin but not yet in the promised land: the new creation, where, as Revelation 21 v 23 tells us, we will have no need of the sun or moon because the presence of God will forever be the light by which we see. When the Holy Spirit was given to the apostles, he came with flames at Pentecost. Unlike those early believers, we don't see him as literal light before us, bright tongues or a pillar of fire; but God *is* with us now in our dark places, guiding us with the lamp of his word and by the light of his Spirit.

When we cannot find our way out of the cave, and David's words in Psalm 139 v 11 could be ours—"Surely the darkness shall cover me, and the light about me be night"—we must cling to what the psalmist declares to be his lamp and his light: the word of God (Psalm 119 v 105). We must lament, voicing the questions that will give way to the truth we most desperately need: that "even the darkness is not dark to [God]; the night is as bright as the day, for darkness is as light with [him]."

As we voice our discontent, doubt, and desire for relief, may the rich promises of God's word give light to our eyes, so that we can see his goodness, even as we grieve. May we be filled with hope enough to lament to the One who is with us in the dark.

**READ:** Psalm 13; Psalm 88; Lamentations 3 v 16-24

**REFLECT:** What have you done with your negative feelings in the wake of your loss? Have you stuffed them down? Have you voiced them to friends? Have you prayed them to God?

Which lines in the verses above are most relatable to you? Why? How do these questions or complaints reveal an underlying faith in who God is, even amid sorrow or confusion?

**RESPOND:** Write out your own lament. Consider writing one of the passages above in your own words and incorporating your own experience.

 **JOURNAL**

# Praying Our Fears

Miscarriage was the sort of thing that only happened to other people. Then it happened to me. After being caught completely off-guard in that ultrasound room by the death of our baby, my body felt sort of stuck in "fight or flight." I lived in a state of readiness, feeling as if I were seconds away from tragedy at every moment. All of my imagination, which had been so positive—wondering who this baby might be, or how he or she might bring joy to our family—became negative, churning out worst-case scenarios so as not to be caught off guard again. *What else might I lose? How else might I experience pain? Where am I vulnerable or unprepared?*

My anxiety made it difficult to enjoy time with my toddler. I was nervous behind the wheel of my car. I held on to my husband for a few moments longer before he left for work each morning. Intimacy became difficult because risking becoming pregnant and miscarrying again felt too scary. Each time my phone rang, I worried that it would be bad news about a family member.

Miscarriage showed me that I was not immune to suffering or loss. And I was afraid.

David had plenty of reasons to be afraid, and he often was. The book of Psalms contains several songs he wrote while hiding in caves from men who were seeking his life. In those songs, David offers us a framework for dealing with our fears. One such psalm is Psalm 27. Here we find him in the same sort of darkness that he describes in Psalm 139 v 11, crying out to God, calling him "light."

> *The Lord is my light and my salvation—whom*
> *shall I fear? The Lord is the stronghold of my*
> *life—of whom shall I be afraid? —Psalm 27 v 1*

In the midst of the darkness, tense and troubled, David tells himself the truth. In the next few lines of the psalm he names his fears specifically (the wicked advancing to devour him, an army besieging him, and war breaking out against him), and applies the truth about God's character and his promises to each of them.

"Do not fear" is the most common command in Scripture. I memorized a few of these verses to "claim" in those moments when I was gripped with dark thoughts about the future or present unknowns. I sought to eradicate my fears using Bible verses like mallets in a whack-a-mole arcade game. Philippians 4 v 6: "Do not be anxious about anything." Matthew 6 v 25: "Do not be anxious about your life." Luke 12 v 32: "Fear not."

But my fears kept popping up. I felt shame over my lack of courage—over my lack of faith.

But God did not intend for us to use those phrases to eradicate anxiety by our own effort. They are meant to deepen our trust in the Lord as we experience his help. David's language in Psalm 27 hints at this deeply personal aspect of God's care and guidance: "The Lord is *my* light and *my* salvation ... the Lord is the stronghold of *my* life" (emphasis mine). And the passages from which I plucked those fear-fighting verses are deeply personal as well. The tone of my own counsel to myself to *get it together* or to *not let my mind go "there"* stands in stark contrast to Jesus' language in Luke 12 v 32: "Fear not, little flock." *Little flock.* He addresses his followers gently, with language that reminds us of what we are: sheep. But that language also calls to mind who he is: the One to whom we belong, the Good Shepherd.

We are sheep. On our own, we really are as weak and defenseless as in our worst moments we imagine ourselves to be. This humbles us. We fear because we don't know, we can't be everywhere at once, we aren't in control. And in as much as it offers us a reminder of who we really are, our fear is a gift. In that posture of humility, aware of our own lack of knowledge and control, we can receive the remedy for our fears—laying them at the feet of our Good Shepherd, the One who *is* all knowing, who *is* everywhere present, who *is* totally in control. This is where we go to get peace.

God knows how it all shakes out, where it all leads, what the purpose is. You don't; and that's okay because you know *him*. From his word you can know who he is and all that he has promised. He has not said that your life will be free of trouble, that you will never miscarry again, that those you love will not die, or that if you have enough faith, you'll be safe from earthly harm. But he has promised to be *with* you, that he will work all things for your good, and that eventually you will be free from the threat of everything you fear.

This was the remedy for David's fear—not the mallet of platitudes but the comfort of God's promises and presence:

> One thing I have asked of the LORD, that will I seek after: that I may dwell in the house of the LORD all the days of my life, to gaze upon the beauty of the LORD and to inquire in his temple.
> —*Psalm 27 v 4*

This act of gazing upon the beauty of the Lord reorders our affections. Our fear about a great many things grows smaller as our desire for and security in this "*one* thing" grows. Come what may in our earthly lives, our relationship with God and our future in him are fixed and secure. As we seek his face and feast on his promises, our hearts, like David's, are reoriented from focusing on all we are afraid of losing to gazing upon the beauty of what we have: God himself.

David's instruction to his soul to "be strong and courageous" in the final verse of this psalm is nestled between the repeated instructions to draw near to God. So, when your courage is thin, and when your heart pounds within your chest and your mind races as if you are ready to run, choose to run to Jesus, your Good Shepherd. As you peer into the future, which is dark and unknown to you, take hold of and be calmed by the knowledge that even the darkness is as light to him, and that the light of his presence is already there.

**READ:** Psalm 27; Psalm 61 v 1-3

**REFLECT:** What are you afraid of? How do your specific fears reveal what you love? What aspects of who God is do you find most comforting when you consider your specific fears?

Is there a friend you could voice your fears to? Ask them to pray for you.

**RESPOND:** Talk with God honestly about what you are afraid of. Each time you have an anxious thought today, tell it to God and ask for his help and peace.

 **JOURNAL**

# He Will Hold Me Fast

A few weeks ago we visited the ocean as a family. My husband hates the sand, and so I always take lots of pictures to document the rare occasions when he braves the beach. As I scrolled through the images on my phone back at our house, I paused to laugh at one. In it, my three-year-old is suspended in midair with just his big toes in the water. His eyes are clenched shut, his cheeks swollen with the big gulp of air he stored in preparation for being pummeled by the rogue wave now beneath him. His arm is stretched by the weight of his body dangling from his tiny hand, which is held by my husband, who clearly jerked him upward to keep him from going under and being lost in the wave.

Can you imagine if, after the wave had passed, my three-year-old had looked up at my husband and said, "Wow! Good thing I was holding onto your hand, Dad"? That would have made us laugh, because it would have been ridiculous. My son was held above the wave not because he held onto his father but because his father was holding onto him.

You are in that same place: "*Even there* ... your right hand shall hold me" (Psalm 139 v 10).

In the sort of darkness that David describes in these verses—and in the valley of the shadow of death through which you are now walking—sometimes our grip on God doesn't feel so sure. Our palms may sweat with anxiety and fear, our shocked and tired minds might struggle to claim truths we never thought to doubt before, and our hearts may feel cold and distant from God.

There is a connection between our bodies and our minds and feelings. Having just lost an unborn child and quite a bit of blood, reeling from tragic and shocking news, women who have miscarried are not at their best, intellectually or emotionally. In that sort of spiritual darkness, in a time when nothing makes sense and when our doubts seem to be speaking louder than our faith, we must remember that believing is not a matter of strength. Faith is not something we conjure up; it is a gift we receive. And the One who gives us faith is the One who keeps it going.

The powerful conclusion of Jude reminds us of this:

> *To him who is able to keep you from stumbling and to present you blameless before the presence of his glory with great joy, to the only God, our Savior, through Jesus Christ our Lord, be glory, majesty, dominion, and authority, before all time and now and forever. Amen.*
>
> —Jude v 24-25

Notice that first phrase: God "is able to keep you" not because of your grip on him but because of his grip on you.

Jesus himself describes the power of this grip:

> *My sheep hear my voice, and I know them, and they follow me. I give them eternal life, and they will never perish, and no one will snatch them out of my hand. My Father, who has given them to me, is greater than all, and no one is able to snatch them out of the Father's hand.*
> —*John 10 v 27-29*

Here, again, we find the relief of embracing the reality that we are sheep. Jesus says that not one of his sheep will be lost, not because they are savvy and loyal but because he is a protector and keeps them close. Just as we learned a few days ago in Psalm 23, his rod is a comfort because it protects us; and his staff is a comfort because it keeps us near to him, pulling us close when we're prone to wandering off. Nothing can pluck us from his hand—not our lack of intellectual fortitude and not our lack of emotional resilience. My dear sister, you are kept.

John Piper writes to the one who is afraid of their unbelief:

> *It is utterly crucial that in our darkness we affirm the wise, strong hand of God to hold us, even when we have no strength to hold him ... The darkest experience for the child of God is when*

*his faith sinks out of his own sight. Not out of
God's sight, but his. Yes, it is possible to be so
overwhelmed with darkness that you do not know
if you are a Christian—and yet still be one.*
*—When the Darkness Will Not Lift, page 38*

I'm always encouraged in my own experiences of spiritual weakness when I remember Peter. Though Peter claimed at the Last Supper that he was "ready to go with [Jesus] to prison and to death" (Luke 22 v 33), he went on to deny Jesus three times before the morning. In spite of his zeal, he would fail. Jesus knew this, and yet he also assured Peter that he would be kept: that he was praying for him and that he would strengthen him. And Jesus' prayer for him was answered—Peter went on to live a life of zealous faith and die the death for Christ that he had claimed to be ready for. My sister, as you fight the fight of faith with weak arms and a faint heart, Jesus is praying for you as he prayed for Peter. He knows your frame and has so much compassion for you (Psalm 103 v 14). You may doubt or falter, but that doesn't mean your faith has failed or your soul is lost.

That is why, even as we lie awake with all of that heartache, weakness, bitter disappointment, and fear—even as we sit in the darkness, riddled with confusion and doubt, wondering if we will make it out of this with our faith intact—we can say with the writer of Psalm 16 v 7-8, "I bless the Lord who gives me counsel; in the night also my heart instructs me. I have set the Lord always before me; because he is at my right hand, I shall not be shaken."

You shall not be shaken: not because you are strong, not because you are sure, but because God is at your right hand. Because his right hand holds yours.

**READ:** Romans 8 v 16; John 10 v 11-18, 27-30

**REFLECT:** How has your experience of miscarriage, shock, and grief affected your faith? What things about God, if any, have you doubted, which you never questioned before?

What do you think would have been going through Peter's mind as he heard Jesus' words about his failing faith? How would you have responded? What comfort do you draw from this story?

**RESPOND:** *When I Fear My Faith Will Fail*
(Ada Ruth Habershon)

*When I fear my faith will fail,*
*Christ will hold me fast;*
*When the tempter would prevail,*
*He can hold me fast.*

*He will hold me fast,*
*He will hold me fast;*
*For my Savior loves me so,*
*He will hold me fast.*

 **JOURNAL**

## LAUREN WASHER

# My Losses and My Gains

I heard my dad on the phone to my husband ask whether or not I was conscious. That's the last thing I remember before waking up on the bathroom floor, covered with a towel, hearing my husband telling me the ambulance was on the way.

"I want to have more babies," I whispered through my tears. I already had two daughters, but I was sure the complications from this miscarriage would result in the death of my lifelong dream to have a large family.

Sometimes I feel like I'm not allowed to grieve my miscarriages, because my prayers were answered and God enabled me to become pregnant several times again after that scary day. My home is now filled with six vibrant children. Sometimes it seems that because God granted the desire of my heart, I don't have permission to feel sorrow over my losses—as if the babies we never met are unimportant or insignificant.

After my first miscarriage resulted in an emergency hospital stay and a month-long recovery, I knew the reality of both physical and emotional suffering. Even though I have given birth to two sons and two more daughters, I also experienced complications from another miscarriage shortly before our last child was born; and each pregnancy was marked by the nagging fear of another loss. We've rejoiced over the babies placed in our arms, and we've also wept over the babies we never got to hold.

I often hold back from talking about my experiences when I hear women who struggle with infertility sharing about their repeated miscarriages or their inability to conceive. I'm hesitant to enter the conversation because I don't fully understand. I can't relate to the woman who is unable to carry a baby to full term. I will never identify with the woman who spends years seeing fertility specialists and emptying her bank account only to be told that the chances of a healthy pregnancy are slim to none. I won't experience the agony of coming home from the hospital and staring at an empty crib.

But I do know the pain of losing what you hoped for.

I know the embarrassment of blood seeping into your pants and rushing to the bathroom before it becomes too obvious. I understand the trauma of being taken to hospital in an ambulance. I've felt the misery of delivering a dead child into a toilet. My uterus has been poked and prodded in order to remove all remnants of a failed pregnancy.

Miscarriage is awful. I still cry over the emptiness in my arms from the babies I loved but never knew.

Yet greater than any understanding I may or may not have of another mom's experience is a confidence that

God is intimately acquainted with my babies, my story, and my grief.

God formed all eight of my babies, and even though the lives of two of them were brief, every beat of their tiny hearts mattered. Because they were created in God's image, my babies have dignity, worth, and tremendous significance. We absolutely remember their lives—with gratitude and love.

Although I don't share my miscarriage stories with each hurting mom I encounter, I'm certainly able to empathize with her. I can listen, weep, and serve her in tangible ways that I believe will be helpful.

As for my grief, well, I continue to realize that I'm allowed to feel that too. I've learned to bring my raw emotions to the Lord, and I've experienced the gift of his presence in the midst of my pain. The psalms—particularly Psalm 18 and Psalm 71—have provided both instruction on how to voice my lament and a deeper understanding of God's unwavering faithfulness when life doesn't make sense. I've found great comfort in God's ability to tenderly and compassionately minister to my heart. In the darkest moments of grief, I cling to the reality that Jesus gets it. He understands intense physical pain. He has experienced unbearable emotional suffering. He carried all of our grief and felt every bit of our sorrow when he suffered and died on the cross. There's truly no greater comfort than this.

God allowed me to have the big family I always wanted. I don't deserve it, but I'm grateful: for my children, yes, of course, but mostly for the way God continues to reveal his glory in both my losses and my gains.

Our gains will never undo our losses, but both serve to point us to the One who chose to lose everything in order for us to gain more than we could ever imagine.

*For you formed my inward parts;*
*you knitted me together*
*in my mother's womb.*
*I praise you, for I am fearfully and*
*wonderfully made.*
*Wonderful are your works;*
*my soul knows it very well.*
*My frame was not hidden from you,*
*when I was being made in secret,*
*intricately woven*
*in the depths of the earth.*
*Your eyes saw my unformed substance;*
*in your book were written,*
*every one of them,*
*the days that were formed for me,*
*when as yet there was none of them.*
*How precious to me are your thoughts,*
*O God!*
*How vast is the sum of them!*
*If I would count them,*
*they are more than the sand.*
*I awake, and I am still with you.*

**PSALM 139 v 13-18**

# Shame Over Grief

I wanted one more ultrasound. Just to be sure before I took measures to help my body recognize what had happened.

The technician measured the baby again. A little over half an inch. This little one's body had been housed within mine for twelve weeks. There should have been a tiny face, and tiny legs and arms. The size and shape were confirmation; the baby had definitely died. The doctor came in and ran her finger back and forth over the section of the screen displaying this tiny body. "As you can see," she said, "no baby. Just a fetal pole." I recognized the shift in the language she was using. She was trying to help me disconnect from this little one—to help me let go. I choked back my tears.

A week later, after using medication at home, I came back in for another ultrasound. "Looks good," the doctor said, moving her finger in a circle around the part of the screen showing the lining of my empty uterus. "Nice and clear. You passed all the products of conception." Again, I choked back tears. I felt a strange tension: I was glad there would be no need for further intervention, but I mourned the emptiness of my womb—the absence of my baby, whom my doctor lumped in with "products of conception." I left the obstetrician's office with an empty womb and empty hands.

When I reached my house, I found within my mailbox a package from my sister: a tiny silver ring, just 2 millimeters in diameter, on a dainty 18-inch silver chain.

It was crafted by a silversmith who makes a ring for each of his grandchildren when they are born. If one of his daughters miscarried, he would present her with a tiny ring like this, affirming the personhood of the child she had lost—the grandchild he had lost. My sister purchased one for me, to affirm the personhood of the child I had lost—the niece or nephew she had lost. As I rolled this ring between my finger and thumb, the tears that I had choked back in shame hours before now flowed freely in sorrowful sobs.

When an unborn baby is referred to with words like "fetal pole," "clump of cells," or "product of conception," it's hard not to feel silly about your tears. Comments like "At least it was early" or "At least you weren't very far along" provide a subconscious scale for the appropriate measure of sorrow you're allowed to feel. An abortion culture that dehumanizes life in the womb in order to justify ending unwanted pregnancies leaves little to no room for a woman to grieve the child she loses to miscarriage. At every turn, we are told that the loss we feel so acutely isn't much of a loss at all.

The words of verses 13-16 of Psalm 139 offer sweet validation to those of us who feel deep sadness over the loss of the tiny babies in our wombs. The God of the universe affirms there the personhood of these children. These beautiful words declare the significance to him of life in the womb—the life of the child you carried in *your* womb.

The Creator of heaven and earth was the active Creator of your child. That little embryo developed and grew under the attentive eye and careful hand of God the Father, who formed all of his or her inward parts and knitted together his or her tiny form. The frame of your child was not hidden from God when he or she was made in the secrecy of your womb. The eyes of God saw the unformed substance of your baby, and in his book was written each significant day that he purposed for his or her brief life. Though this tiny person never lived a day outside of your womb, he or she was made in the image of God and had purpose and dignity. The loss of the life of a person is always worth grieving.

The state of New York passed a law earlier this year that does away with criminal penalties for self-abortion and defines "person," when referring to "the victim of a homicide," as "a human being who has been born and is alive." This human-made law implies that unborn lives are not people; that their destruction is of no consequence. But the living God declared otherwise in the law he gave to his people. In Exodus 21 v 22-25, he calls for retribution when violence to a pregnant woman causes the loss of the life in her womb. God values the life of the unborn child.

If abortion culture or society's dismissive reaction to this type of "early" loss have caused you to feel that the magnitude of your grief means that something is wrong with you, let this collection of verses from Psalm 139 massage your aching heart, just as the sentiment behind that tiny ring massaged mine as I rolled it between my fingers. There is no shame in grieving the loss of a life—the loss of a child. You have every right to weep. This is not simply the disappointment of a dream or the death of an imagined future; those things would themselves give reasonable cause for sorrow, but you are grieving more than that. You are grieving the death of a person.

The Bible's affirmation of personhood in the womb is also beautifully displayed in the story of Jesus. The miracle of the incarnation—of God becoming man—began at Jesus' conception, when the Holy Spirit caused life to be created in the womb of a virgin. The one in whom and through whom all things hold together was held within the body of a young girl. The Prince of heaven took on flesh as a tiny embryo, knit together in secret. The Gospels record Jesus' relative John the Baptist leaping within the womb of his mother when Mary came to visit her: one unborn child recognizing the deity of the other (Luke 1 v 41). And just as God determined the number of your baby's days in sovereign wisdom, he determined the days of the life of Jesus as well. The Christ-child was conceived and was born to live the life we could never live, to die the death we deserved, and to be raised to new life—so that one day death would be no more.

So grieve freely, sister, as you mourn the life of this baby. Grieve without dismissing or minimizing your reaction, but do not grieve without hope.

**READ:** Luke 1 v 39-44; Jeremiah 1 v 4-5

**REFLECT:** Have you felt that your grief was disproportionate to the gestational age or size of your child? How do these verses impact those feelings?

**RESPOND:** *Father, you are the Creator of life and the Creator of the life of the baby I miscarried. Please help me to grieve without shame by helping me share your perspective on the preciousness of life. Thank you for your plan of redemption, which began with conception. Thank you for Christ, whose finished work enables me to grieve with hope.*

**JOURNAL**

# Fearfully and Wonderfully Made

*"I just can't seem to understand Psalm 139 anymore."*

It wasn't exactly the response I expected to hear when I asked my friend Ruthie how she was doing. Her daughter had just been told that the baby girl that she was carrying would not be able to survive outside of the womb. "Fearfully and wonderfully made?" she went on. "This just doesn't seem wonderful. This seems like a mistake." She was wrestling with how or why God would form her grandchild's body without several vital organs.

Many friends of mine who have miscarried have had doctors offer them the explanation that this type of loss often happens when the body recognizes a chromosomal abnormality. But I've also had friends who have been told after testing that their multiple miscarriages were the result of an "inhospitable womb." For some, a biological condition causes their body to tragically and mistakenly treat life in the womb as a foreign threat; for others, their bodies simply don't produce enough progesterone to sustain a pregnancy, and so their babies cannot survive. Many of us don't know what caused us to miscarry, but this much is clear: in order for a miscarriage to happen, something has to go wrong. Every woman I have ever talked with about her miscarriage has described feeling as if her body had failed her somehow, or as if it had betrayed her.

I must admit, Ruthie's question about David's words in Psalm 139 puzzled me as well. Could I insert my name or the name of my unborn baby into this psalm? Can we say that our babies were wonderfully made if a chromosomal abnormality made it impossible for them to live? Can we declare it over our own bodies even if they have proven to be "inhospitable" or are filled with eggs that could never develop into healthy babies?

It may be helpful to look at the meaning of the words that David uses in verse 14. In the original language, the word "fearfully" can be translated as "revered," and the word "wonderfully" can be translated to mean "separate" or "distinct." The nuance is similar to the English word "distinguished," which we use to mean both "important" or "illustrious" and "different." So, we could rephrase this statement, based on David's language, to say that life in the womb is both awe-inspiring and distinct. But what does this actually mean? Let's look at each of these words in turn.

First, "fearfully." According to this verse, every human life, whatever its shape or duration, should produce a sense of amazement. Sperm meets egg, cells divide—conception is a delicate and intricate process.

Even when the loss of a baby occurs almost immediately after a positive test is taken, all that has taken place since conception is magnificent. My own miscarriage allowed me to hold in my hands and examine an entire system that had been built within my body from a part of my husband and a part of myself. Though it was disturbing and upsetting to see a sac and placenta outside of my body at this stage, it also moved me to worship in amazement at God's design.

Beyond the amazing and complicated process by which you can read the words on this page, think about all that your body is doing as you sit at rest right now—your lungs inflating with air, your heart circulating blood, your nerves sending messages to your brain that enable you to feel this book in your hands. Considering all of these processes should inspire awe in us, just as we would be amazed by a gorgeous sunset or hearing the kind of live crescendo performed by a full orchestra that causes the hair on our arms to stand on end. *Awe.* We should be in awe at the way in which we were created—the way we were designed.

Second, "wonderfully"—separate, distinct. All human life is beautifully set apart from the rest of creation because it images God, even though that image has been fractured by the fall. You and your child were set apart from the rest of creation as humans: bearers of God's image. But you were both also distinctly made as individuals:

designed to be you, not anyone else. Your life is not a mistake. And regardless of whether or not you intended to conceive, the life of your baby was not a haphazard accident either. God is sovereign over all life at every stage. He is in control of every detail about you—your personality, your appearance, your eye color—and every detail about your baby, whether known or mysterious to you. You were uniquely crafted and perfectly designed to carry out the purpose for which God created you. That purpose might not be clear to us, but this mystery doesn't make David's words any less true.

Even as we experience shame and guilt over our imperfect bodies as we suffer the effects of the fall, we can still say with the psalmist that we, and our miscarried babies, are fearfully and wonderfully made. Ultimately this is not because of who we are, or who they were, but because of who our Creator is: a fearful and wonderful God; one who inspires awe and wonder; one who is distinguished from every other as the only living God; and one of whom we are told over and over throughout Scripture that there is "none like him."

Though we long for the perfect bodies we will gain in the new creation, we can learn the liberation of praising him in the "not yet" by confessing that we, and the babies we carried, are indeed fearfully and wonderfully made. It is an exercise of faith to say with David, "I praise you," even as we wait and groan for redemption.

**READ:** Genesis 1 v 1, 27, 31; Romans 8 v 18-25

**REFLECT:** Have you felt failed by your body in miscarriage? Have you felt that the life of your baby was an accident or a waste? What about your own life?

**RESPOND:** Spend some time talking with God about why it may feel difficult to call yourself or your baby "fearfully and wonderfully made." Ask him to align your perspective with his. Praise him for his creative power and wisdom.

 **JOURNAL**

# Wonderful Are
# Your Works

When David considers God's intimate involvement in his own creation, he is moved to worship. "Wonderful are your works; my soul knows it very well." Those might not feel like words that you would imagine yourself saying in this less-than-ideal situation, where it's easier to see the difficulty than the beauty and provision. But meditating on the work of God is perhaps even more important in the midst of suffering, when it's not as easy to make out.

Psalm 143 is another psalm where we find David considering the work of God's hands. But he's not in a broad place or on a mountaintop overlooking beauty. He is being pursued and pressed by the enemy. From that place of trouble, he writes in verse 5:

> *I remember the days of long ago; I meditate on*
> *all that you have done; I ponder the work of*
> *your hands.*

In Psalm 40, we meet David again considering the works of the Lord while he is surrounded by "troubles without number" and "overtaken" by his sin (Psalm 40 v 12). There he declares:

*You have multiplied, O Lord my God, your*
*wondrous deeds and your thoughts toward us;*
*none can compare with you! I will proclaim and*
*tell of them, yet they are more than can be told.*
*—Psalm 40 v 5*

In the midst of overwhelming circumstances, David pauses to remember the days of long ago and meditate on what God's hands have done. Even in his longing for God's saving help, he is able to say, "The Lord is great!"

Up until this point, the devotions in this book have focused specifically on the difficulty you are now walking through. We have zoomed in on you and your current circumstance. But now we are going take a cue from David in these psalms of distress and zoom out.

"Ponder the work of [God's] hands" (Psalm 143 v 5). You can begin by looking up and looking around. See the work of God's hands in the created world.

It's cold and raining as I type these words in a friend's seaside apartment. Beads of water are rolling slowly down the outside of the window, and a vignette of condensation has formed on the inside, framing the view of an ocean covered by thick fog. But if I try, I can make out the waves crashing on the South Carolina coastline, pelicans diving and dipping into the water, and beach grass blowing in the breeze beneath that low-hanging cloud. There is beauty, even though it's difficult to see.

This beautiful creation is God's work. It is worth pausing to observe it and worship him for it.

I also consider the kind eyes and gentle hands of my husband. I imagine the voice and gait of a dear friend of mine whose laugh and posture I love. Their bodies and personalities, as Psalm 139 reminds us, are God's work. These created beings are worth thinking on and praising him for.

Remember his faithfulness in "the days of old" (Psalm 143 v 5). Beyond the created world, consider the work of God's hand throughout all of history. Think of his promise of redemption in Genesis 3 v 15. Think of the covenants he made with Noah, Abraham, and Moses. Remember how he delivered his people in the book of Exodus. Think of the promise he made to David—that a king with a never-ending kingdom would come through his line. Think of all the names in the genealogy of Jesus in Matthew 1 v 1-17 and the way that God worked in their lives. Think of his faithfulness to the early church in the book of Acts and in the lives of the authors of the New Testament.

"Meditate on all that [he has] done" (Psalm 143 v 5). Remember the virgin birth. Consider the miracles of Jesus in the Gospels: who he touched and how they were healed. Remember how he cast out demons and raised the dead, and how he humbled himself to serve. Remember Christ's death. Recall his resurrection and his ascension.

Recall his "wondrous deeds" (Psalm 40 v 5). Now zoom back in a little. Zoom back in and think about the work of God in your own history. Consider his providential hand in your own life. Remember how God has drawn you to himself and how he has been faithful to you.

And now zoom all the way back in to your current circumstance. The life that was conceived in your womb was the work of God's hands and is worth thanking and praising him for. Your own body and distinct personality, intricately and purposefully created by him, are worth thanking and praising him for. Your life, fully known and designed by him, is worth thanking and praising him for.

Consider, too, the work of God in the past month. Where have you seen his faithful hands, even in the smallest of ways and on the hardest of days?

Think of his "thoughts toward us" (Psalm 40 v 5). We can worship and praise God for so many things. Greatest of all is the work he accomplished for us on the cross: the finished work of Jesus, which secured for us an eternity where we will be free from suffering and pain, and all that is now mysterious will be plain and clearly praiseworthy.

The posture we assume when we declare that God's works are marvelous gives us the perspective to see, and to praise him for, the work he is doing now, even if it's hard to make out through fog and rain-covered window-panes. So, even as your mind may doubt when your circumstances don't seem wonderful at all, declare with your mouth what your soul knows very well: "I praise you ... Wonderful are your works." And in that posture, you can find rest and relief, as David did, in thanking God for the work he has done, the work he is doing now, and the work you know he will complete.

**READ:** Ephesians 1 v 7-14; Psalm 111

**REFLECT:** Make a list of created works that are obvious and easy for you to declare to be "wonderful."

Spend some time reflecting on how God has worked in and through you in ways about which you can confidently say, "That work in my life was wonderful."

**RESPOND:** Pray through Psalm 111. Feel free to pause and insert into your prayer things you thought of while reading this chapter. If you haven't done so already, praise God for the child he created in your womb.

 **JOURNAL**

KRISTIE ANYABWILE

# The Puppeteer

Spiritual. Not religious. This is how I would have described myself throughout college and early in my marriage. I grew up in the church but didn't really have a relationship with the Lord. So in my college years I created my own version of religion, which was comfortable and completely under my control. I treated life like a puppet—believing that I controlled my own destiny, that my life was in my hands, that I could be and do anything I set my mind to. I pulled the string of success, and the arm of life pointed me toward a career in teaching. I pulled the string of marriage, and the man of my dreams danced alongside me. I pulled the string of family, and a baby began growing inside of me, filling me with hope and joy in the belief that my life as the puppeteer was the best life.

Warm. Jittery. This was the state of my heart as soon as I realized I was pregnant. I was barely six weeks along but I told everybody! Within a couple of weeks, we received a care package of onesies and blankets and bibs from family and friends. I was teaching high school at the time and even told my students so they could share in our joy.

Every day they asked how I was feeling, when I would know if it was a boy or a girl, and why I didn't look pregnant yet. I answered every question with delight. Each night I'd fall asleep reading *What to Expect When You're Expecting*. Things were going exactly as planned. I knew that by now the baby's eye color was established, the fingers and toes were forming, and the heartbeat could be detected. We made an appointment with a well-regarded ob-gyn in our area, and dreamed and planned as we waited to see our little pea-sized wonder on the sonogram and to hear our baby's heartbeat for the first time.

Still. Dead. This was a reality I never would have imagined. As the sonographer meticulously guided the probe around my gel-covered abdomen, we held hands and our breaths waiting to see our baby. I followed along, watching the screen, unsure of what I was looking at. She pointed out the little pea-sized image on the screen: "There's your baby." After a few minutes, she excused herself and brought the doctor in, who continued moving the probe, pressing harder into my abdomen. The room got very quiet and claustrophobic. I worriedly glanced at my husband. The doctor completed her surveying and with icy finality said, "I'm sorry, there's no heartbeat."

What did that mean? Was it too early to hear? Should we make another appointment? She showed us the little pea that should have pulsated with life, but instead lay still as if it was covered with a stack of mattresses. No pulsating pea; no beating heart besides my own, which was now breaking into tiny little pieces, shattering every hope and dream that a master puppeteer could possibly imagine.

Cold. Flat. This was the bed on which I lay and the sound of the doctor's voice when she told me that my baby was dead. Something broke in us as we heard the words from our doctor. No heartbeat. It felt as if she was telling us not only that our baby was not viable but that we were not viable as parents. As grief enveloped us and led us into the darkest cave of depression we'd ever experienced, I wondered why and how this had happened. Soon I was fully enveloped in a crisis of faith as I recognized that a miscarriage was not in my own plan for my life. I wondered, "If I'm not in control, then who is? If there is a God, and he's ultimately in control, then what else might he have planned for me?" The godly influence of my grandma came flooding into my mind, helping me to see that I needed to seek God.

Questions. Answers. As depression made itself at home in our hearts, a television preacher caught my husband's attention. I'd never imagined my husband, a former Muslim, watching a Christian preacher—nor being intrigued by one. The pastor taught the Bible verse by verse, explaining 2 Timothy 2 v 15 in a way we had not been exposed to before. We were drawn to God's word through this preacher's careful expositions, and eventually decided to drive hundreds of miles across several states one weekend to visit the church which he pastored. At that service he preached the gospel from Exodus 32, pointing out the sinfulness of sin and explaining how

God's righteous anger over sin was appeased through the redeeming sacrifice of Christ. For the first time, I understood that I was not the puppeteer of my own life but a sinner in need of the salvation that is offered through Christ. I understood myself to be under the sovereign hand of God, whom I can trust to care for me in my deepest pains. At that church service, both my husband and I gave our lives to Christ.

Acknowledge. Celebrate. I keep a small, gold pendant on my jacket that replicates the size and shape of a 10-week-old fetus. It is a sweet reminder of the baby I lost when I was 10 weeks pregnant. Although I lost that baby 25 years ago, I will never forget that life nor the loss.

I would never have chosen miscarriage for myself or anyone else, but God used that tragedy in my life as the means by which he called me and my husband to himself. That salvation is truly a gift from the Lord.

# What Is My Good?

If I had a penny for every time someone has told me, "Well, you know, all things work together for good," I'd have a full piggy bank. That phrase seems to be the choice brand for Christians when it comes to Band-Aid responses to pain.

These words are borrowed from Romans 8 v 28:

*And we know that for those who love God all things work together for good, for those who are called according to his purpose.*

This verse has been a comfort to me in times of sorrow, but during the days and weeks after we lost our baby, the speculation about what that "good" might mean for me that generally followed the loose, off-hand quotation of this verse wasn't comforting at all. I was assured by many that God was sparing me from greater pain; perhaps a difficult life with a special-needs child or the heart-wrenching experience of raising a rebellious teenager.

These thoughts were as unhelpful as they were unfounded. They also took away any comfort that

Romans 8 v 28 is meant to bring by distracting from its true meaning. These hypotheses all spoke to what my imagined worldly good might be; but this verse isn't about earthly prosperity.

David's words in verse 16 of Psalm 139 remind us of a chief attribute of God: his omnipotence. This means that God is all-powerful. He is sovereign, or in control, over all things. The days that were formed for us were written in *his* book, when as yet there were none of them. God is the author of all the days of our lives. In Romans 8 v 28, this all-powerful God is the one Paul says is working all things for good. It's not about some law of nature, so that we might say, "You know how these things go" or "It all works out in the end." No, the almighty Creator of the universe, who holds the stars in place and tells the ocean how far it may come, also ordains your days and the events of your life.

However perplexing the question may be of how a good and loving God could allow suffering, his control is a comfort to us in hardship because we know his character and his promises to us. This verse from Romans is one of the Bible's most beautiful promises to the sufferer. God is not only at work in all things; he is working for the good of those who love him. If that is you—if you are one who loves God—then you can rest assured that he is using everything that happens in your life for your ultimate good. Miscarriage is not good, no, not good at all, but according to the Bible, God's purposes for you within it most certainly are.

Though often neglected, the two verses that follow verse 28 are crucial if we are to rightly interpret and apply it and determine what those good purposes are:

> *For those whom he foreknew he also predestined to be conformed to the image of his Son, in order that he might be the firstborn among many brothers. And those whom he predestined he also called, and those whom he called he also justified, and those whom he justified he also glorified.* —Romans 8 v 29-30

These two verses remind us that God has been working for our good since before time began, to save us from our sins and reconcile us to himself. But they also show us that when God's word tells us that he works all things together for our good, that good isn't necessarily our material or physical good—the growth of our families, for example. He is committed to our spiritual good.

I heard a friend say just yesterday that "the greatest moments of our lives are not necessarily the happiest ones, but the ones that cause us to rely more fully on God." Our greatest good is fellowship with our Father. As we experience him more, we love him more; and as we love him more, we start to look more and more like Jesus. This is one of God's glorious purposes in pain: he uses our trials to make us more like Christ. This process, called sanctification, prepares us for the joy of glorification, when we will be perfect in the fullness of the presence of God.

James cites this as the reason to rejoice during hardship: the testing of our faith produces perseverance, which will one day make us complete and mature and not lacking in anything (James 1 v 2-4). I don't know about you, but my experience of miscarriage showed me very clearly a great deal of what I lacked: faith, courage, strength, understanding, and self-control. I long to be perfected and lack none of these things.

When James says that the process by which we are perfected is one of "testing," he isn't referring to some type of academic exam. This word is used to describe the purification process of fine metals. The heat of a fire melts the metal and causes impurities to rise to the surface, where they can be skimmed off the top.

God uses the painful fire of suffering to refine and purify us. Though miscarriage exposed my lack, I have seen God use it to make me more like Jesus, to increase my trust in him, to give me endurance, to grow me in wisdom, and to transform my prayer life.

Joni Eareckson Tada, who lives with quadriplegia and who has endured an extraordinary amount of pain and suffering, once said, "God permits what he hates to achieve what he loves" (*When God Weeps,* page 84). My sister, God loves having fellowship with you. He loves conforming you to the image of his Son. He is working to that end. This is the greatest good he could give you—and it will outlast any merely earthly good you can imagine.

**READ:** Romans 5 v 3-5; James 1 v 2

**REFLECT:** Can you think of examples in the Bible when God used earthly hardship to bring about spiritual good? How about in the lives of people you know?

How have you seen him at work within you through this experience? How is he exposing and transforming you?

**RESPOND:** *Oh! To Be Like Thee*

(Thomas O. Chisholm)

> *Oh! to be like thee, blessed Redeemer,*
> *This is my constant longing and prayer;*
> *Gladly I'll forfeit all of earth's treasures,*
> *Jesus, thy perfect likeness to wear.*
>
> *Oh! to be like thee, oh! to be like thee,*
> *Blessed Redeemer, pure as thou art;*
> *Come in thy sweetness, come in thy fullness;*
> *Stamp thine own image deep on my heart.*

 **JOURNAL**

# Nothing Is Wasted

Hours before the appointment at which I was told that our baby had died, I threw up. The nausea that accompanied this pregnancy came on strongly around five weeks, and I continued to throw up for weeks after the baby had left my body. I had forged ahead through all of the vomiting in the weeks prior, telling myself, "It will all be worth it in the end." But the end had come much sooner than I expected, and there was no baby. Instead, there was just a bloated belly and lingering symptoms—symptoms that felt pointless, and even cruel.

I've heard this frustration expressed by many women walking through miscarriage. With no baby to bring into the world to raise and love, they feel as if their money, time, and pain have been wasted.

Are you feeling as if things are a waste in this season? Perhaps it's the energy you put in to preparing for this baby. The money you spent on doctors' visits, ultrasounds, or infertility treatments. The maternity clothes you bought. The time you spent trying to conceive or the time that is passing now while you wait to be able to try again.

The weekend you spent recovering instead of hanging out with friends. Or the painful symptoms you got from the medication that didn't work and left you still in need of the D&C you wanted to avoid?

Has anything left you wondering, "What's the point?"

Sometimes we work harder to trust God with the bigger things, like death and tragedy, than we do with the details—the seemingly tangential things which, like flea bites, just leave us cynically swatting and frustrated. I wonder if David may have been wrestling with this thought as he wrote verse 16 of Psalm 139. He could have just stated that God ordained the days that were formed for him and left it at that, but instead he adds the aside, "every one of them." The complete sovereignty of God is a comfort to us in this place where we feel as if certain days or details have no purpose. The truths from Romans 8 that we explored in the previous chapter help us remember not only God's purposes for our pain but also the parameters of those purposes. God works *all* things together—from the most bitter and painful to the seemingly pointless—for good. No day, no detail, occurs outside of the scope of his redemptive purposes.

You're not alone if you've been asking this question from a place of fatigue and cynicism. After all of their suffering, Job and Jeremiah both went as far as questioning why they were even alive, cursing the days that they were born (Job 3 v 3-10; Jeremiah 15 v 10). But their lives were not a mistake. God used them not only to communicate his character amid their suffering to their contemporaries but also to form whole books of Scripture. Through both of their lives, God displayed his glory. He is doing the same thing with your life.

An understanding of God's purpose and plan brings comfort to us in our pain because it brings perspective. In 2 Corinthians 4 v 17, Paul uses the words "light" and "momentary" to describe his own (extensive) suffering. These are probably not words you would reach for to describe the hardship you are currently enduring—those weeks I spent throwing up because of a pregnancy that had already ended certainly didn't feel light or momentary—but Paul doesn't use those words to say that his suffering is insignificant. We know this because in Romans 8 he has been talking about those same "sufferings of this present time" (v 18), when he states that God works *all* things together for good (v 28).

No, nothing is wasted or insignificant: not the life of your baby, not your lingering symptoms, not the time that's passing—none of it. Paul's use of the words "light" and "momentary" are not intended to minimize our pain but to lift our gaze within it. Earthly afflictions feel heavy now, but they are nothing compared with the eternal glory we are being prepared for.

God is using every detail of your experience surrounding miscarriage for your good and for his glory. When we consider this truth, difficulty that has felt endless and pointless starts to feel purposeful and easier to bear, as we embrace the knowledge that, somehow, it will enhance our future joy.

When you doubt this, think of the story of Joseph. His older brothers despised him, sought to kill him, and ended up selling him into slavery. Then he was thrown into prison for a crime he didn't commit. The story is heart-wrenching. But in the end, Joseph boldly stood before the brothers who had betrayed him and declared, "You meant evil against me, but God meant it for good" (Genesis 50 v 20). No day of Joseph's life was outside of God's control, and every detail was used by God for Joseph's good and for his own glory. Joseph ended up in a powerful position within Pharaoh's court; more significantly, God used this to preserve his people through a famine. In doing so, he ultimately guaranteed the survival of the family line that would one day lead to Christ, the One who will bring us to glory.

Your pregnancy may have ended in death rather than birth, but it was not "all for nothing." Every detail is being used for good—your greatest good. I don't pretend to understand exactly how this works, but somehow, God's redemptive purposes for your life are being accomplished through the suffering you're currently enduring. He's getting glory from it, and you're being prepared for glory by it. So the next time your weary soul asks, "What's the point?" answer the mystery with this assurance: "Even this. Even this, God is using for my good and his glory."

**READ:** Genesis 50 v 15-21; 2 Corinthians 4 v 16-18

**REFLECT:** Write out Romans 8 v 28. After "all things," add "—even" and list the things that have felt like a waste to you in this season.

**RESPOND:** Be honest with God about your frustration over the good things that have been lost and the hard things that still remain in the wake of your miscarriage. Ask him to help you to believe that he uses all things for your good and for his glory.

 **JOURNAL**

# Feeling Guilty or Responsible

*"Was it my fault?"*

Prenatal-care instructions draw a straight line from our bodies and decisions to the health of our babies. We're told to avoid eating soft cheeses and drinking alcohol. We're instructed not to exercise too rigorously and to stay hydrated. We're counseled to take a daily prenatal vitamin with plenty of folic acid. The burden of responsibility that accompanies motherhood starts long before a baby is born. So, when the death of a baby occurs within a mother's body, this is the sort of question that haunts us as we mull over things we did or didn't do, or feelings we did or didn't have.

I remember so clearly my doctor placing his hand on mine, looking into my tear-filled eyes, and saying, "This is not your fault." His intention was to offer comfort, but I remember wondering how he could say those words with such certainty when he knew so little about me, my past, or my actions during this pregnancy.

Just as my doctor couldn't tell me the reason behind my miscarriage, I cannot possibly know the reason behind yours. Yet whether or not my doctor's statement was true, the sentiment behind it was absolutely correct. There is no point in being consumed by guilt over your miscarriage.

Of greater comfort than these scripted words from a physician with limited knowledge are the words of Scripture—the word of the God who *does* know all things, who is in control of all things, and who has the authority to forgive and to offer full assurance of pardon.

David's declaration in Psalm 139 v 16 tell us that God knows all the days of a baby's life before he or she is even formed in the womb. He alone is sovereign over life. So you can let yourself off the hook. There is nothing you could have done to lengthen or shorten the number of days that God ordained for your baby in his sovereign wisdom. Though this life came to be within you, you did not create it. You are not all-powerful. But your completely good and infinitely wise God is. And his goodness and wisdom mean that his supreme power is a great relief as we consider the death of our unborn babies.

Even if your pregnancy came sooner than you expected or before you felt ready, even if you didn't intend to *have* children or to have any *more* children or to have more children quite *yet*, even if you were secretly afraid of what pregnancy might do to your body—your thoughts and feelings are not powerful enough to change the days that the God of the universe numbered for your baby. And neither are your actions.

Perhaps you suspect that your miscarriage is some sort of punishment for past sin. Maybe you suspect that God is withholding motherhood from you now because you had an abortion as a teen, or you didn't wait until you were married to have sex. If this is you, hear this assurance of pardon: your Savior bore the full weight of your sin on the cross. If you are in Christ, there is no punishment left for any sin you commit—past, present, or future.

Punishment aside, if you believe that your miscarriage was a direct consequence of a sinful decision you made, God's word offers relief for you too. My dear guilt-ridden sister, regardless of whether or not you are at fault, you can find full and complete forgiveness in Christ. For any guilt you feel—if upon careful thought you conclude that you are right to feel it—you can experience the relief that comes from repentance. Tell it to Jesus and rest in his extravagant grace. There is no need to harbor guilt over something for which the Judge of all the earth has promised to forgive you. There is no reason to sit in shame when you are fully accepted by the God who knows all your actions and has also searched and known all the thoughts and intentions of your heart (Psalm 139 v 1-4).

In John 9, Jesus and his disciples encounter a blind man, and the disciples ask, "Rabbi, who sinned, this man or his parents, that he was born blind?" (v 2). They assume, in accordance with the popular belief of their day, that his blindness is the direct result of wrongdoing.

But Jesus directly refutes this view: "It was not that this man sinned, or his parents, but that the works of God might be displayed in him" (v 3). For the blind man, "the works of God" meant the miracle work of Jesus; for us, it could mean any number of things. The point is that God uses tragedy in the lives of his people—even tragedies that *do* arise from their own sinful decisions—to display his glory. The disciples' question was concerned with responsibility and fault, but Jesus' response reveals the more important question and more relevant answer: what is the purpose of God, and how will his works be displayed in your experience of miscarriage?

When you are tempted to claim responsibility for the death of your baby, you can give God glory by acknowledging his sovereignty over life, praying and proclaiming verse 16 of Psalm 139. When you feel bitterness and confusion over the mystery of suffering, you can give God glory by trusting that his plans are perfect and his ways are higher than yours, even if they are incomprehensible to you (Psalm 139 v 6). And when you feel despondent and sorrowful, you can give God glory by hoping in Christ. He suffered for the sins of his people so that his Father might receive glory, and so that as you consider the life of your baby, and the events and days of your own life, you might clearly perceive that the actions and glory of God are inextricably linked to your good.

**READ:** Job 2 v 3; 4 v 7-8; John 17 v 1-4

**REFLECT:** Have you replayed the events of the last few weeks and wondered what may have caused the death of your baby? Has anything led you to feel guilty or responsible?

How do Psalm 139 v 16 and the truth of the gospel offer you comfort in this place?

**RESPOND:** Spend some time giving God glory by praising him for his sovereignty over all things. Voice your questions to him and talk to him about the things you believe or are tempted to believe might be the reason for your baby's death. Ask him to assure you of Christ's atoning work and to help you to walk in freedom from guilt as you grieve.

 **JOURNAL**

## JESSALYN HUTTO

# The Staircase

The nurse and I go through the usual ritual: urine sample, weight, blood pressure, temperature, and then checking the baby's heart rate—except this time the ritual is brought to a halt by the sound of uninterrupted static. As she moves the doppler wand over my swollen belly, the nurse's face becomes more and more concerned.

"Sometimes I can't find the baby," she says with a forced calmness. "We'll send you over to the ultrasound technician, and he can get a better look."

In that moment my heart fights to believe that the technician will be able to find what the nurse cannot, while my brain attempts to prepare me for the inevitable. *At 17 weeks a baby should be easy to find. He or she is no longer the size of a lima bean. They should be turnip-sized.* As my husband and I are led through the waiting room, I hold back the instinct to throw up.

In the darkness of the ultrasound room my worst fears are realized. The uninterrupted static of the doppler speaker is traded for the motionless black and white outline of a baby girl on a screen. Static. Motionless. My heart begins to imitate my womb and the tears roll down my face. She measures fifteen weeks. For two weeks she has been resting peacefully within my body. There, but at the same time not there. *How did I not know?* I can hear my husband let out a sob beside me.

Soon we are sitting, waiting. Our faces are red, puffy, and snot-stained amid a sea of couples awaiting good news about their little ones. I feel their stares, full of curiosity and pity, and silently wish to be anywhere but here.

As my husband answers a call from his mother, I stare with laser focus at the metal staircase ahead of me. My doctor will be ascending it at any moment—or at least I hope she will. My mind races with a million thoughts. *Did I do something to kill my baby? Did one of my other children bump into my belly too hard a couple weeks ago? Why would God finally give us a girl only to take her away?* But mostly I wonder what a late-term miscarriage will look like. Our family anticipated finding out the gender of our baby today, but now we will return with the devastating news that our first little girl is already a memory.

My mind races back to another time when I sat and stared like this in a doctor's office. It was three years ago, and I was naïve. I hadn't known the risks. I hadn't known that my body could just as easily miscarry the children within me as it could nurture and bring them to full term. I was a first-time mom and filled with all of the hopes and dreams that the daughters of Eve are meant to have for their children. I had not yet learned the painful reality that was the result of our first mother's sin. I had not yet tasted the death that sin brings with it.

According to the pregnancy books, there could have been a whole host of reasons for the blood that should not be staining my undergarments. My heart clung to these best-case scenarios. On that occasion it wasn't a staircase I was staring at but a poster for a seminar that the office was hosting. My mind tried its hardest to focus on the poster rather than the fear threatening to overtake my body. My foot tapped nervously as its words and images began to blur behind a wall of tears.

When the doctor heard that I'd been spotting, she sent me straight to the ultrasound technician. It was the same experience I would have three years later: a dark room and a stranger giving me the worst news of my life. The baby wasn't measuring eight weeks like it should. No heartbeat.

And yet, they offered, there was still *some* hope. Our dates could be off. The baby could be younger than we previously thought. We would just have to wait and see. The doctor sent me home to do the waiting, with little preparation for what I would see if the worst came to pass.

That baby was delivered at home. The delivery of his or her tiny body was the most painful thing I had ever experienced. Looking back, I'm glad that it was so painful, because the physical pain matched the anguish of my spirit. I was a mother whose child was being ripped from her body without her consent.

Now, as I face the prospect of another miscarriage, I can't help but remember the pain associated with the first.

Is God really asking me to experience that physical and emotional agony all over again? *Oh God, why?*

But even as the words quietly exit my mouth, a wave of calmness washes over me. I think back to those horrible days and remember that the Lord did not abandon me. Even in my darkest hour, as I was curled up in a fetal position, experiencing the contractions of labor for a baby the size of a lentil, the God of the universe drew near to me. He entered into my darkness and held me fast. Yes, three years ago, submerged and drowning in the deep waters of grief, I learned to tether myself to the eternal Anchor, Jesus Christ.

*Will he not do the same for me now?* Staring at the staircase before me, I know the answer to my question. Jesus is the same yesterday and today and forever. He will not forsake me. Though my heart is filled with fear and uncertainty, there is one thing I can know for sure: my God *will* be with me. And that is enough.

# The Bigger Story

*"You know, it's just so common."*

Every time I heard that response to our miscarriage, I cringed a little. Lumping the story of the brief life of a precious child in with the lives of so many other unborn babes who died in the womb wasn't much of a comfort. It felt invalidating. It felt dismissive. Sure, "1 in 5 pregnancies end in miscarriage." But my baby wasn't a number; my baby was a person. This wasn't just a pregnancy loss. This was the loss of a child.

The fact that it is common doesn't make miscarriage, or infertility for that matter, any less sad or confusing. Walking with friends through this season of trying to have babies, losing babies, and celebrating gender reveals and births, I have often thought that I might deal the fertility cards a little differently if I was holding the deck. I remember feeling so confused shortly after our loss as I was working with a ministry that provided support for teen moms. Most of these girls conceived accidentally and were struggling to provide stability for their babies;

at the same time, many of my friends who were married and fervently praying for children either couldn't conceive or were suffering multiple miscarriages.

Those of us experiencing pain and sorrow over loss and longing for children find ourselves in good company as we read the Bible. The cards are dealt similarly in Scripture: mysteriously and seemingly unfairly. Sarah, even after being promised a baby, waits well beyond her childbearing years to conceive; but her slave Hagar conceives by Sarah's husband immediately (Genesis 16; 18 v 1-15). We find further hardship and pain over childbearing or infertility in the lives of Rebekah, Leah and Rachel, and Hannah. But we can make sense of these stories because we can see all of their expressed purposes play out in the Bible.

When we read the Bible as one big story, we see how the experiences of each of these women contribute to a larger narrative of redemption. Elderly Sarah gave birth to Isaac at the perfect time for him to grow up and meet his wife, Rebekah. After years of infertility, Rebekah gave birth to twins: Jacob and Esau. Jacob married sisters who fell into conflict with one another over infertility and childbearing. One of them, Leah, gave birth to Judah, from whose tribe Jesus would come. The other, Rachel, gave birth to Joseph after years of infertility; he was born at the perfect time to preserve the people of God and the line of Christ in famine. (These stories are told in Genesis 21; 24 – 25; 29 – 30; and 37 – 50.) In the book of Samuel, Hannah's weeping prayers for a child were answered with the birth of a son. He became the prophet who anointed

King David, who was the one to receive the promise that a Messiah would come from his line whose kingdom would never end. And all that led to perhaps the strangest story surrounding childbearing in the Bible: Mary, an unwed virgin, became pregnant with the Savior of the world.

These stories echo what David's words in verse 16 of Psalm 139 proclaim: God is sovereign over life in the womb, over all of our days, and also over all of history. The days of these women and their children were ordained by God—every one of them—when as yet there were none of them. Their stories were recorded in a physical book, but even if the book David references is not literally real, the image helps us to make sense of our own stories of waiting and frustration. We don't always have the luxury of knowing the specific purposes behind God's responses to our own longings for children or our fervent prayers to preserve the lives of the babies in our wombs.

But, though our longings and losses occur in a different context than the history contained within our Bibles, they are still a part of the story told within it: the story of redemption.

The story began in Genesis with God's beautiful and good creation. Then sin and death entered the world through the disobedience of Adam and Eve, and so God's people suffer. Our suffering in childbearing is a part of that story—the curse of sin pronounced in Genesis 3—but it isn't the end of the story. God sent Jesus to suffer as well so that death would be defeated finally and forever. The Bible doesn't just tell us about history; it shows us how God is at work in the story. As we endure the mystery of suffering surrounding fertility, we can have every confidence that although our stories may not be part of the story culminating in the birth of Christ, they are just as intentionally written by God to accomplish his purposes in the story of the redemption of his people (think of sanctification, mercy ministry, or evangelism). God is not a part of our story so much as we are a part of *his*.

Yes, the sorrow and pain surrounding childbearing is common; but that's not where comfort comes from. Placing ourselves in the company of these Bible women isn't valuable because we see that this struggle has been common for thousands of years, but because we see that the same God has been faithfully weaving together the stories of his people for his good purposes since the beginning of time. He is no less at work in your life now. And though we may not be able to see the purposes of our own stories as clearly, we do know how God's story ends. The women in the Old Testament had the hope of a coming Savior. We have the hope of heaven because of the finished work of Jesus. The story of your life and the story of your family are being written by the Author of all of history. As mysterious as the details may seem now, the conclusion is beautiful and sure.

**READ:** Ephesians 1 v 3-10; 1 Samuel 1 v 1 – 2 v 11

**REFLECT:** Consider for a moment your view of God and the purpose of your life. Do you think of him as a part of your story, or do you think of yourself as a part of his? What leads you to that answer?

How do Hannah's words in 1 Samuel 2 reveal her concern for the greater story, rather than the story of her family?

**RESPOND:** Write out the ways in which you relate to Hannah and/or the other women mentioned in the story of Scripture. Ask God to help you to see your story, and the story of the formation of your family, in terms of his story.

 **JOURNAL**

# A Word for Difficult Dates

One of the joys of learning that I was pregnant with our second child was the discovery that a few of my dearest friends were expecting babies with due dates close to mine. But after the loss of my little one, the joy of sharing pregnancy with those friends became a hardship. Each time I heard one of them reference how many weeks they were, I would automatically calculate how far along we would be if our baby had continued to grow. These subconscious thoughts fell like rain on seeds of bitterness.

My first period came. *I shouldn't be bleeding. I should be pregnant.* We talked about "trying again." *I shouldn't be having this conversation. I should be due in November.* Friends announced pregnancies. *My second child should be older than theirs.* Our first child aged. *My babies should be 21 months apart.* Another cycle. *I shouldn't be releasing another egg. I should still be growing a baby.*

"Should be." These are words that plague the woman who walks forward after loss.

In a perfect world—one where Adam and Eve had not sinned—there would be no death and no loss. So, no, this is not what God designed for the world: in that sense, none of the stories we hear of death, sickness, hardship, and loss *should be* happening. The reality is that we now live in a fallen world; but, however difficult it may be to understand, God is still sovereign over it. He still holds the pen that writes our stories. David affirms that reality in Psalm 139 v 16: "every one of them." God ordained the day when we unknowingly conceived, and he ordained the day when our baby prematurely left my body. He ordained the day of my first period thereafter. He ordained each day that has passed since our loss and the days of the future we are walking into.

He is fully in control. But we must also remember that he is fully good.

A card still hangs on our refrigerator, which a friend made for me when she learned of our loss. On it, she hand-lettered Psalm 145 v 13-19:

> *The LORD is faithful in all his words*
> *and kind in all his works.*
> *The LORD upholds all who are falling*
> *and raises up all who are bowed down.*
> *The eyes of all look to you,*
> *and you give them their food in due season.*
> *You open your hand;*
> *you satisfy the desire of every living thing.*
> *The LORD is righteous in all his ways*
> *and kind in all his works.*

> *The LORD is near to all who call on him,*
>   *to all who call on him in truth.*
> *He fulfills the desire of those who fear him;*
>   *he also hears their cry and saves them.*

This psalm proclaims God's complete control, but also his character and care. When I put this card up, I didn't need a reminder that I wasn't in control (our miscarriage proved that to me full well). But each morning as I opened our fridge, this psalm helped me to rest in knowing who was in control: the Lord, who is *trustworthy, faithful, wise, benevolent,* and *righteous* in *all* his ways and in *all* he does. The Lord, who is *near*, who *hears*, and who *saves*.

The knowledge of God's complete control, coupled with the knowledge of his character and care, should influence the way that we experience and talk about the passing of time and the difficult dates that follow our losses. It should help us move from the third and fourth stages of grief to the fifth—from bargaining and depression to acceptance—acknowledging, however reluctantly, and embracing, however uncertainly, the sovereign and perfect will of our good Father for our families.

If we do this, we may still say "would be," but we will no longer be plagued by "should be." I marked that shift in my journal about eight weeks after our loss:

> *If our baby's heart had not stopped beating,*
> *I would be about 20 weeks now. I would*
> *undoubtedly be wearing maternity clothes.*

> *I would likely know his or her gender. But God,*
> *in his love for our family, allowed our baby to*
> *leave my womb at what would have been 12*
> *weeks. If I truly stop and consider his character*
> *and love for his children and the knowledge*
> *of his sovereignty, I cannot continue to use the*
> *language "should be."*
>
> *If I was supposed to be 20 weeks pregnant, I would*
> *be. But I am not. This is the lot God has given our*
> *family, and trusting him means embracing the fact*
> *that our present reality is what "should be" because*
> *it is what is.*

The "definite plan and foreknowledge of God" also involved Jesus' death (Acts 2 v 23-24). The Son of God suffered alongside us as well as for us, so that one day all that was lost in Eden can be restored—not just to what it was but to something even greater than what *would be* had God's children listened and obeyed. The moments when you have said, "This is not how it's supposed to be," point to a longing for that eternal day when all will be as we have felt that it *should be*. God promises that day of restoration. And we can trust him to deliver.

In the days, weeks, months, and years ahead, you will experience markers for the baby you lost. Many specific dates ahead may be difficult because they look so different from what you expected. But we must remind our grieving, protesting hearts on those days—which are not as we imagined they *would be*—that they are in fact as they *should be,* because there is no better place for us than within the will of God.

Even as you grapple with the words *should be* and *would be,* set your hope on the certainty of what *will be.* Cling to the finished work of Jesus, which has secured your inheritance, finally and forever.

**READ:** Acts 2 v 23-24; Psalm 145

**REFLECT:** What events or interactions have been reminders of how far along you "should be" or "would be" if you had not miscarried? What future events or dates do you anticipate serving as markers to remind you of your loss?

Draft a sentence or two that you can say to yourself in those hard moments or on those difficult dates.

**RESPOND:** *Whate'er My God Ordains Is Right*
(Samuel Rodigast)

> *Whate'er my God ordains is right:*
> *his holy will abideth;*
> *I will be still, whate'er he doth,*
> *and follow where he guideth.*
> *He is my God; though dark my road,*
> *he holds me that I shall not fall:*
> *wherefore to him I leave it all.*

## JOURNAL

# Weeping With Those Who Weep

A friend of mine recently miscarried in much the same fashion that I had. The parallels were uncanny, really. And in a situation where I might have minimized her pain, done nothing, or felt unsure a few years earlier, I now knew what to do. I knew what to ask and how to listen. I knew what to say, and perhaps more importantly what not to say. It was easier to imagine what she might be feeling because I had been in her situation. It was easier to think of ways to comfort her because I had been comforted in that place.

Beyond the similarities of this situation, I have found that since the loss of our baby, I am better able to offer the comfort of the Lord to people who are suffering all kinds of pain, because our miscarriage forced me to develop a theology of suffering and to learn to see God's goodness within it. This book in your hands is an extension of his comfort to me. It has been a sweet, redemptive gift for me to write it and even share portions of it with friends who have lost babies in the womb as I have been writing.

A comfort we can draw as we read David's words declaring that God has planned each day of our lives is that God has ordained purposes for our pain. Though we cannot know all of them, according to the apostle Paul, one purpose is that this experience of loss will make you better able to comfort others. Consider his words to the church at Corinth:

> *Blessed be the God and Father of our Lord Jesus Christ, the Father of mercies and God of all comfort, who comforts us in all our affliction, so that we may be able to comfort those who are in any affliction, with the comfort with which we ourselves are comforted by God.*
> *—2 Corinthians 1 v 3-4*

Paul says that because you are being comforted by God in your affliction, you are able to comfort others in any affliction. The comfort you will be able to provide to the suffering people you encounter won't come from perfectly understanding their suffering, but from the experience of God's comfort during your own suffering.

During my own miscarriage, the person who offered me the greatest comfort had never lost life in the womb, but she had recently experienced the tragic death of her mother and grandmother, besides enduring her little sister suffering from cancer and her grandfather having a limb amputated. She ministered to me through her presence; through helping me with tasks in the home; through listening; and through sharing books and verses that had helped her reconcile God's goodness with her own suffering. She never compared my grief to her own beyond saying that suffering was suffering, however the degree of trauma may vary.

The power to comfort doesn't come from the ability to say, "I know exactly what you're feeling!" or "I know exactly what you need." It comes from knowing what it feels like to suffer, though no experience of suffering is exactly the same; and from knowing what it feels like to be comforted by God in suffering. We are not good comforters because of our ability to share our own pain and declare our own solutions, but because of our ability to empathetically share someone else's pain and declare the goodness of God to them through word and deed.

So what does this clearly stated purpose for your pain mean for you on this day, as your wounds still feel fresh? Today, you should experience and take in the comfort that God is providing for you. This is the time to bask in that comfort, to drink from it deeply: his grace and peace; his loving care expressed through others; encouragement from his word; the ongoing beauty of the created world; nuggets of wisdom from sermons and books. In all the places where you are tasting and seeing his goodness, chew and savor it. And on the day when someone you know is in a bitter circumstance, you will be able to help them to taste the sweet comfort of their heavenly Father in that place.

Your suffering has many purposes, but in this one, you have the comfort and humble honor of knowing that you are being prepared to be used by God as a better-equipped minister to the broken. Because you have experienced his comfort, you will be able to comfort others. I praise him in advance for the ways in which he will use the painful particulars of your loss, enabling you to care for your neighbors with the same comfort with which he has comforted you.

**READ:** 2 Corinthians 1 v 3-5; Romans 12 v 15

**REFLECT:** How have you experienced the comfort of God in the wake of the loss of your baby?

How do you imagine you might now be better equipped to care for someone who is suffering? Does anyone specific come to mind?

**RESPOND:** Thank God for the specific ways in which he has comforted and cared for you in this season. Ask him to help you to drink deeply from the well of his comfort today, so that you will be able to pour out his comfort on those who are hurting around you tomorrow.

 **JOURNAL**

COURTNEY REISSIG

# Miscarriage and the Frowning Providence of God

Pregnancy has always been a bittersweet experience for me. We lost our first baby through miscarriage after a few short weeks in my womb. After two years of surgery, medicine, tests, and begging God for a child, God graciously gave us the twins. But my pregnancy with them wasn't easy either, leading me to deliver them eight weeks early.

We love having children and longed for more, but from that first miscarriage onward, we entered pregnancy with a slight hesitancy. We knew how it could end. We knew how uncertain it could be. The innocence had been lost for us.

It was with that cautious fear and expectant hope that we began walking through another pregnancy when our twins were nearly a year old. In mid-January we were overjoyed at the news that God had given us another life. We were so excited to see the twins with a sibling so close in age to them. But we were nervous. Would this pregnancy proceed as planned? Or would it unexpectedly end? Would it be complication-free? Or would I face another difficult pregnancy? Early on we learned that my progesterone was low, which only heightened our fear. But we also felt a calm that only the Lord could provide. We had seen him walk with us through so much already, and we wanted to trust him completely with this little one he had given us.

Pregnancy symptoms came on early and with full force, leading us to believe that all was well. We scheduled our first appointment and went to the hospital on a cold February Monday, fully expecting to see our wiggly, 9-week baby on an ultrasound.

But that was not to be.

I knew something was wrong when the ultrasound tech took longer than I was expecting. With the twins, she had found the two of them within seconds. This time she struggled to find even one. Within minutes our worst fears were realized. The baby had never fully developed, only the sac. Essentially, all along my body had only been thinking that I was growing a baby—which explained all of my pregnancy symptoms.

To say that we were heartbroken is an understatement. Miscarriage is so ugly and so raw. It takes the hopes and dreams of expectant parents and dashes them on an ultrasound table or the bathroom floor. It takes something that should bring the greatest joy and ushers in the greatest pain. Even if you are prepared for loss, it is always a shock and a grief.

We were comforted by the truth that God never lets us go. When your body can't hold on to a baby, what other hope do you have than to cling to the God who will hold on to you? The loss of our fourth baby was not a surprise to him. He is a good and loving Father, who walks with us through even the darkest of days.

I found a familiar friend in the hymn-writer William Cowper, who was no stranger to dark days. He wrote these lyrics:

> *Judge not the Lord by feeble sense,*
> *But trust Him for His grace;*
> *Behind a frowning providence*
> *He hides a smiling face.*

Miscarriage is a "frowning providence." We know God is in control, but it doesn't feel good.

Yet as we weep, God weeps. As we grieve, God grieves. As we beg for faith, he grants it. As we grasp for hope in the dark, he is shining light through.

Sometimes he does this through flesh-and-blood people who have walked the same road as us. I found one such person at the checkout counter in my local pharmacy.

"It doesn't get any easier, does it?"

You meet kindred spirits in some of the strangest places sometimes. In the weeks following our second loss, I needed medication to complete the miscarriage. It's not a happy trip to the pharmacy: I was nervous, thinking how I would explain why I was purchasing the very same medicine that is used for a chemical abortion.

No one tells you how awkward that will be.

But then something sweet happened. After the pharmacist left, the pharmacy tech continued to finish my order. As she processed my credit card, she mouthed the words "I'm sorry." She went on to tell me how she also had had two miscarriages, and confirmed my feelings that this really doesn't get any easier.

She understood. She had been there. And she validated my grief and my fears. The Lord met me with comfort even through a process that brought me much dread.

Her words have stayed with me in these many years since we lost our fourth child. In many ways her words are very true. But they are also a reminder to me that sometimes the "smiling face" of God that shines behind his frowning providence comes in the form of people you don't even know. Sometimes he shows up and ministers to his weary people in his word, and sometimes he does it in the drugstore checkout line.

As I've walked through miscarriages, infertility, and life-threatening pregnancies, I have quickly learned that there is nothing easy about living in this sin-cursed world. The stain of sin is all around us. If it were easy, then this would be our home. Our hearts know that one day this will all be made right and we will understand God's purposes behind it all. Right now we only see darkness, but our hearts tell us there is light coming. And that is what we cling to. With tears in our eyes and lumps in our throat, we are begging God for more faith through this dark valley of loss.

And we trust him.

> *The Lord has promised good to me.*
> *His word my hope secures.*
> *He will my shield and portion be*
> *As long as life endures.*     *—John Newton*

# Rooting Ourselves in God's Word

In the past few devotions, we've taken a closer look at the sovereignty of God. We've thought more about who he is as the Creator, the One with authority over life and circumstances, the One who wastes nothing in working all things for our good, and the Author of redemptive history. All this moves David to write verse 17, where he speaks about God's thoughts. *Strong's Hebrew Dictionary* defines the word translated "thoughts" in the ESV as "purposes" or "aims." When the psalmist considers the purposes and authority of God, which we have acknowledged in these reflections, he is moved to exclamatory lines of worship.

The sum of God's purposes is too vast to number. Can you even imagine trying to count the grains of sand on a seashore? We see the same point again in the phrase "I awake, and I am still with you" (Psalm 139 v 18). David implies that the providence and creative power of God are inexhaustible, going beyond sleep and even death. The seventeenth-century commentator Matthew Henry says of this verse, "God's counsels concerning us and our welfare are deep, such as cannot be known. We cannot think how many mercies we have received from him." In Romans 11 v 33 we hear Paul echoing David's sentiment as he declares, "Oh, the depth of the riches and wisdom and knowledge of God! How unsearchable are his judgments and how inscrutable his ways!"

But the limitations of our minds and the inexhaustibility of the character and conduct of God are not a reason to give up meditating on God. David calls the thoughts and purposes of God "precious." The writer of Psalm 119 expresses the same idea—and to him God's purposes are especially precious in suffering. In one section, he essentially has nothing to hold onto and is overwhelmed with sorrow, but he describes God's word as the source of his life and strength even in desperation:

> *My soul clings to the dust; give me life according to your word! When I told of my ways, you answered me; teach me your statutes! Make me understand the way of your precepts, and I will meditate on your wondrous works. My soul melts away for sorrow; strengthen me according to your word!*          *—Psalm 119 v 25-28*

He even goes so far as to say that he is glad for his affliction because it has caused him to cherish God's word more deeply:

> *This is my comfort in my affliction, that your promise gives me life … It is good for me that I*

*was afflicted, that I might learn your statutes.*
*The law of your mouth is more precious to me*
*than thousands of gold and silver pieces.*
　　　　　　　　*—Psalm 119 v 50, 71-72*

*Precious.* There is that word again. God's word and God's thoughts are precious to the psalmist because he sees them as the source of his life, his counsel, his strength, and his delight, in the midst of that deep, personal suffering.

In times of trouble, when our minds are tired, our bodies are weak, and our souls are weary, we may feel as if we don't have the energy or capacity to invest in reading God's word. But according to the psalmist, the times when we feel as if we are melting away or have nothing to cling to but dust are the times when we need the word of God the most.

The Bible is God's revelation of himself. It tells us who he is, who we are, and how we are to live. It contains the good news of the gospel and the promises of God, which we can cling to with certainty when circumstances feel scary and the future uncertain. When we are suffering, the Holy Spirit uses the word of God to protect us by presenting the truth; he renews our minds, making our thoughts more like God's thoughts and aligning our hearts with his will, and soothes our hearts, making us more comfortable with mystery as we become more convinced of God's wisdom.

So even and especially in hardship, we, like the psalmist, must root ourselves in God's word, asking for understanding by the power of his Spirit so that we might be protected from disordered thinking, and held up and renewed by the truth.

You've been doing that as you've been reading this devotional, which hangs on Psalm 139. But before long, it will conclude. Then what? How do you continue planting yourself in Scripture? Maybe reading your Bible feels intimidating or you don't know where to begin. But it doesn't have to be fancy. I would recommend beginning with one of the Gospels or letters and reading straight through a few verses at a time, asking the Spirit of God to give you understanding. Observe what the text says and pull out what it reveals about God and about the world or humanity. Find something you can praise God for, and something you can take away as a challenge for yourself.

When I was young, my parents took me to my first 3D movie. At the door to the theatre, we were each handed a pair of paper glasses with two differently colored plastic lenses. As the film started, my head began to ache as my eyes were inundated with blurry images and fuzzy collections of pixels. Clumps of light swarmed around on the screen. Then I put my glasses on, and I saw clearly, even vividly. I was able to make sense of what had seemed fuzzy before. Rather than fighting off a headache for the next hour and a half, I was able to enjoy the unfolding of a well-written story.

Scripture is like those glasses. All of life is meant to be interpreted through its lenses. God has offered you his word to help you see clearly so that you can join the psalmist in meditating on the works, ways, and wonders of God. For us, as for the writers of Psalms 119 and 139, it is our daily bread and the light by which we see.

**READ:** Matthew 4 v 4; Hebrews 4 v 12

**REFLECT:** How have you experienced the words of the Bible helping you to see your circumstances more clearly or accurately? Have you experienced being strengthened by it in a time when you might have otherwise withered? As a starting point, which parts of Psalm 139 have been most helpful to you in this season?

**RESPOND:** Thank God for his word. Ask him to help you to make time to study and get to know it. Pray for his help in understanding your circumstances through it.

 **JOURNAL**

*Oh that you would slay the wicked, O*
*God!*
*O men of blood, depart from me!*
*They speak against you*
*with malicious intent;*
*your enemies take your name in vain.*
*Do I not hate those who*
*hate you, O LORD?*
*And do I not loathe those who*
*rise up against you?*
*I hate them with complete hatred;*
*I count them my enemies.*
*Search me, O God,*
*and know my heart!*
*Try me and know my thoughts!*
*And see if there be*
*any grievous way in me,*
*and lead me in the way everlasting!*

**PSALM 139 v 19-24**

# A Cry for Justice

Despite the popularity of the words "fearfully and wonderfully made," I doubt you'd ever find this portion of Psalm 139 written in a hand-lettered font on a sweatshirt or a coffee mug. At first glance, these words don't feel appropriate, let alone comforting. After the beautiful, poetic phrases we've just read, words like "loathe" and "complete hatred" are jarring, to say the least. David is calling for the blood of his enemies. But aren't we supposed to *love* our enemies?

This portion of Psalm 139 earns it a place among those in the category of "imprecatory" psalms. These psalms profess hatred for the enemies of God and call for him to execute righteous judgment on evil. Jesus himself, the perfect man, referenced and acted to fulfill one of them—Psalm 69 (John 2 v 17; 15 v 25; 19 v 28-29).

It's important to recognize that David's words are uttered against God's enemies and leave judgment in God's hands. It is his zeal for God and his desire for justice that motivate his strong language. Though reading these words might make us uncomfortable, we can certainly relate to and embrace the psalmist's sentiment as we consider the ultimate enemies of God: evil and death.

You've doubtless felt anger and outrage at death in the wake of your miscarriage, after feeling its sting within your own body. Perhaps you've felt a burning desire for justice as you consider abortions from the vantage point of a mother who has felt the unwanted loss of life in the womb. But anger is an emotion that many of us are quick to assume is ungodly. That is why we feel discomfort upon reading David's words.

Yesterday I spoke with a friend of mine whose baby died in her womb at 23 weeks. Her due date is this week, and after sharing her frustration over how different this day looked than she had imagined, she criticized herself for being angry. But as David shows us, anger is a justified response to seeing and experiencing the results of the fall.

This outrage is a feeling familiar to your Savior as well. When Jesus showed up at the tomb of Lazarus two days after his death, we are told that he was "deeply moved in his spirit and greatly troubled" (John 11 v 33). Because this verse precedes the sentence "Jesus wept," I always took "deeply moved" and "troubled" to mean that he was just really sad. But in the days following my own miscarriage I studied this passage intently, using several commentaries, and learned that these words actually imply vehement anger over death. Jesus shuddered in outrage at the enemy that is death, as he looked upon the weeping of Lazarus' sisters and their company beside the tomb of his friend.

Nevertheless, it seems that Jesus is two days too late to prevent the death of his friend. When he arrives, Martha says, "Lord, if you had been here, my brother would not have died." But that is not all she says: "Even now I know that whatever you ask from God, God will give you" (John 11 v 21-22). And Jesus responds, "I am the resurrection and the life."

In a short time, Jesus would suffer death himself. But his own death and resurrection would ensure the defeat of death altogether, finally and forever. Revelation 20 v 14 names death as one of the enemies that will be cast into the lake of fire in the final judgment—"The last enemy to be destroyed is death" (1 Corinthians 15 v 26).

We know the outcome of the story—but we still experience godly anger and sorrow. Jesus knew he was about to raise Lazarus, and still he felt outrage; still he wept. But our anger must be directed against death and the results of the fall, not against God himself. He is our ally, not our enemy. We must feel anger along with him, not at him. He is still good. He is still for us.

We may have thoughts that echo Martha's sentiment in saying, "If you had been here…" Yet we know that even though God, in his sovereign wisdom and love, has allowed us to experience loss, he has also given Jesus the authority to crush death. Even if it feels as if he is too late or wholly absent, in fact he sees and knows and is right on time. The day of justice is coming.

As Jesus reminds Martha in John 11, and Paul reminds us in 1 Corinthians 15, death doesn't get the final say—Jesus does. And until that final day when death is destroyed, in our frustration and outrage over death—even amid our lamenting cries of "How long, O Lord?"—our own imprecatory prayer in the face of death is "Come, Lord Jesus. Come and defeat sin and destroy death. Come and make all things right."

**READ:** 1 Corinthians 15 v 20-28; John 5 v 19-29

**RESPOND:** Have you felt anger over death since your miscarriage? How does Jesus' response at the tomb of Lazarus affect your perception of your own feelings?

Does Martha's comment "If you had been here..." seem like faith or doubt to you?

**RESPOND:** *Crown Him with Many Crowns*
(Matthew Bridges)

> *Crown him the Lord of life,*
> *who triumphed o'er the grave,*
> *and rose victorious in the strife*
> *for those he came to save.*
> *His glories now we sing*
> *who died and rose on high,*
> *who died eternal life to bring,*
> *and lives that death may die.*

 **JOURNAL**

# Blessed Are Those Who Mourn

During our experience with miscarriage, it wasn't just the sharp pang of sorrow that made me long to be through that season and on the other side. I wasn't just weary from the sadness; I was tired of myself. I didn't like what grief exposed in me.

Following a miscarriage, a woman's body is weakened by fatigue. Our hormone levels are off, our iron levels are likely low from blood loss, and we are emotionally and mentally exhausted from shock and trauma. Sometimes these factors make it more difficult for us to think before responding or to collect ourselves before reacting. We may be tempted to blame sinful reactions on these physical challenges, but circumstances never produce sin—they simply reveal the sin that is already in our hearts. C.S. Lewis offers a helpful analogy in *Mere Christianity*:

> *If there are rats in a cellar you are most likely to see them if you go in very suddenly. But the*

> *suddenness does not create the rats: it only*
> *prevents them from hiding. In the same way, the*
> *suddenness of the provocation does not make me*
> *an ill-tempered man: it only shows me what an*
> *ill-tempered man I am.*       —*pages 164-165*

The world tells us (and our hearts agree) that grief is a free pass: an excuse to treat people poorly or to behave however we please, releasing us from biblical commands against bitterness, envy, hatred, isolation, or idolatry. Although that invitation to excuse ourselves seems freeing and loving and altogether easier, we miss a beautiful opportunity to enjoy intimacy with God should we accept it.

In verses 23 and 24, the psalmist returns to the language of verse 1 as he invites God to search and know him. David is inviting God to examine his heart and change him. Knowing that we are seen by a loving God should bring comfort, yes; but knowing that he is also holy brings an element of discomfort. When God searches our hearts, he finds things we may wish he didn't know—thoughts and feelings and actions that are not worthy of him. To say "See if there be any grievous way in me, and lead me in the way everlasting" (Psalm 139 v 24) is a true act of worship and honor. This prayer acknowledges our sinfulness in contrast to God's holiness, putting ourselves in his hands and asking for forgiveness and transformation.

However uncomfortable it may be to see and confess our sin, those who do so are ultimately promised comfort. Christ's words in the Sermon on the Mount,

"Blessed are those who mourn, for they shall be comforted" (Matthew 5 v 4), are often quoted in times of sorrow and sadness. But these words also offer comfort to those of us who are grieved by our sinful reactions to painful circumstances. We should read them in the context of the other beatitudes, which focus on righteousness and spiritual things. The people whom Jesus calls blessed are not just those who mourn over the state of a fallen world but also those who mourn the effects of the fall which they see within themselves.

This is a good word for you, sister, if you're longing to be through with this season because of what it exposes in you, or if you are tempted to hate yourself or even doubt your salvation because of the way that you are reacting to suffering.

It is also a good word if you simply don't want to admit your sin. Though you may be tempted to look away or to justify your behavior because you are hurting, choose instead to look to Jesus, who lived the perfect life you never could, who endured suffering without sin as he received the punishment you deserved, and who offers you his Spirit to empower you to walk in a way that is pleasing to him: "the way everlasting."

Psalm 139 v 24 should serve as a reminder of that precious gift for those of us who are in Christ: the gift of repentance. As we see David's example of boldly asking God to reveal his "grievous ways"—his sin—and lead him in the righteous "way everlasting," we remember the forgiveness available to us in Christ and the transforming power available to us in the Holy Spirit. Here we find the confidence not only to face our sin when it is exposed like rats in the cellar, but even, like David, to ask God to reveal it to us.

God often uses hard circumstances to reveal our "grievous ways" to us. But the suffering itself isn't the only painful part of that process. It is also painful to see the parts of us that need to be transformed. In Romans 7 v 24, the apostle Paul cries out from the pain that comes from this kind of sight: "Wretched man that I am! Who will deliver me from this body of death?" But instead of sitting in despair, he answers himself in the following verse with the truth of the gospel: "Thanks be to God through Jesus Christ our Lord!"

Because of the finished work of Jesus, rather than resenting our circumstances for what they reveal in us, hiding from the truth that's been brought to light, or hating ourselves because of our reactions to suffering, we can run to the Father with sorrow over our sin, knowing that he is faithful to forgive and gracious to change us. God is so kind. His exposing of our sin is a grace. He loves us too much to leave us where we are.

**READ:** Romans 7 v 15-25; 1 John 1 v 9

**REFLECT:** How have you responded to seeing your sin during this season?

How does an understanding of the gospel protect us from shame? How does it protect the people around us from us?

**RESPOND:** Spend some time praying the words of Psalm 139 v 23-24, asking God to reveal any "grievous ways" within you. Praise God for the forgiveness and grace to change that he offers in Christ Jesus.

 **JOURNAL**

# What We Deserve

*"Come to Jesus and you'll be rich. All of your
problems will go away."*

This sort of teaching is referred to as the "prosperity
gospel." It promises something to believers during
their lives on earth that the Bible doesn't: perfect health,
abundant wealth, and a life free from trouble.

We might denounce this type of message as false and
dangerous if we heard it from a pulpit or read it in a
book, but in the wake of loss the enemy whispers in our
ears a similar message that's a little harder to dismiss. It's
the same type of subtle suggestion that he whispered
to Eve in the Garden of Eden: *God doesn't want you to
be happy. He's withholding something good from you. You
deserve more. You deserve better.*

How might we experience this line of thinking in the
wake of miscarriage? Perhaps like this:

*"I've done everything he's asked me to do. Why isn't God
giving me a baby?"*

*"I've blessed his name in our loss. If he is going to cause*

*me to suffer, the least he can do is let me miscarry naturally
instead of having to take medicine or have an operation!"*

*"I have sought him through two prior miscarriages. What
is it going to take? Don't I deserve a healthy baby?"*

It is so easy to feel bitter. But bitterness is a "grievous
way." It leads to nothing good.

Ephesians 2 v 1-3 corrects our perspective when we
feel slighted by God. It tells us that we were once "dead
in [our] trespasses and sins ... following the course of
this world" and "carrying out the desires of the body
and the mind." Besides being spiritually dead, we were
"by nature children of wrath."

This is where you and I were before God saved us:
dead and without hope. From the just and righteous
Judge of all the earth, the only thing that we *deserve* is
death. But verse 4 offers perhaps my favorite conjunc-
tion in all of Scripture: "*But* God, being rich in mercy,
because of the great love with which he loved us, even
when we were dead in our trespasses, made us alive
together with Christ."

If God gave us what we justly deserve, we would be
facing eternity in hell, separated from him. But God
offers us mercy in the person of Jesus by *not* giving us
what we deserve. And more than that, he offers us grace:
giving us what we *don't* deserve, making us children of
God, raising us up "so that in the coming ages he might
show the immeasurable riches of his grace in kindness
toward us in Christ Jesus." When we consider that this
is "not [our] own doing" or the "result of works" but

"the gift of God" (Ephesians 2 v 7-9) it becomes difficult to feel bitterness and impossible to feel entitlement.

Imagine you're in a courtroom. A criminal is brought in for sentencing. Rather than condemning him to die, which is what the law requires for the man's crimes, the judge pardons him, telling him that his own son has offered his life in exchange for the man's freedom. The judge then tells the man that he's bringing him into his own family.

Upon entering the judge's house, the man is served pasta. He promptly pushes his plate away in disgust, looks up at the judge and says, "How dare you? I wanted a steak dinner."

That reaction would be almost as shocking as his pardon, and a sign that he had failed to recognize the magnitude of what he had been given. If he understood the mercy and grace he'd been shown, he would do nothing but weep in gratitude, receiving every good thing as a gift he didn't deserve and being content even when what he desired was not delivered.

If you are trusting Christ as your Lord and Savior today, it is because God chose to save you through the death of his own Son when you were by nature an object of wrath, justly deserving his displeasure. Not only that, but God has made you a co-heir with Christ and promised you an eternal life with him in glory. Every other grace you receive is grace upon grace. And you can be assured that whatever he sets before you in this life, he sets it before you in love.

My goal here is not to guilt-trip you into willing yourself to feel more grateful or to beat down your desires with self-deprecating thoughts. Having desires is not sinful. Wishing things were different than the way they are is not wrong. Jesus himself requested that the cup of his sin-bearing work on the cross would pass from him. But his request was followed with a humble submission to God's will.

We, like David, need God to search our hearts, to see if there is any way that we are putting ourselves or our desires before him. We need him to lead us in "the way everlasting" the way that seeks his will, growing within us grateful hearts. Disappointment is inevitable in a fallen world, but the way to stop it from growing into bitterness is through thanksgiving: trusting God's commitment to our good, reminding ourselves of all he has done for us in Christ, and then specifically noticing and praising him for every little thing he gives us as grace upon grace.

**READ:** Romans 6 v 23; Psalm 34 v 8-22

**REFLECT:** Have you been tempted to believe a subtle "prosperity gospel" in the wake of your loss? What, if anything, have you felt God owes you?

How is gratitude for the grace and mercy we have been shown in Christ an antidote for bitterness?

**RESPOND:** *Alas, and Did My Savior Bleed*

(Isaac Watts)

*Thus might I hide my blushing face*
*While his dear cross appears;*
*Dissolve my heart in thankfulness,*
*And melt mine eyes to tears.*

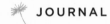 **JOURNAL**

RUTH HATFIELD

# God's Family

Not long after marrying, my husband and I relocated from Australia to the UK. It was an adventure to embrace London as our home. My husband showed me a spreadsheet detailing cultural and historical sites to visit every weekend for the next year. I teased him about life needing more spontaneity, but he explained his reason: wanting to make the most of time before we became parents. He shared my desire that I would become pregnant before too long. I was delighted.

A year passed, and medical tests revealed no identifiable reasons for no pregnancy. Eventually we agreed to try a low-tech, non-invasive fertility treatment: IUI (inter-uterine insemination). We were surprised and thankful to discover that I was pregnant after the first cycle.

Being under the care of a fertility clinic meant early scans were routine. We marvelled at our baby's heartbeat and emailed a scan picture to both sets of delighted expectant grandparents. My mother began planning a visit. We started reading pregnancy books.

My husband felt cautious about sharing our happy news more widely, concerned at how I might cope if miscarriage occurred. But I didn't relate to this perspective. I felt convinced that the length of our developing baby's life was known to God, securely in his hands. If I miscarried, it would be upsetting but not shameful or something outside of God's goodness.

In hindsight I treasure the opportunities I had to share our news with family and friends at a time when it was completely joyful. Those were precious moments of "rejoicing with those who rejoice."

One beautiful Saturday, I was wandering with a friend through Queen Mary's Gardens in Hyde Park, bathed in summer sunshine. I'd reached the eleventh week of pregnancy, but I was becoming increasingly distracted by the onset of symptoms usually associated with a period.

That night my sleep was disturbed by heavy spotting and cramping. I crawled out of bed without disturbing my husband and took advantage of the time-zone differences to phone a friend in Sydney who is a nurse. She reassured me that although bleeding was not a good sign, miscarriage was not inevitable.

Early on Sunday morning I woke my husband and told him what was happening. We notified close friends from church, asking them to pray for us, and then drove to hospital. I was crying as the bleeding steadily increased and we waited to see a doctor.

Having scanned me, the doctor stated succinctly that there was no longer any sign of a baby. I felt a tiny relief that the uncertainty was over. My husband began sobbing. It is still the most grief-stricken I have yet seen him.

I have a medical condition that led to concern about excessive bleeding, so I was admitted to hospital the following day. I recall having to plead that the rigorously imposed visiting hours be relaxed to allow my husband to sit with me and comfort me. I later understood that the cervix dilates for miscarriage, causing pain that can be as excruciating as that of full-term birth, even though a first-trimester baby is tiny.

I felt very empty returning from hospital with no baby. Grief and dismay intensified over the ensuing months as the reality that I'd returned to a "longing to be pregnant" state of existence sunk in. Close friends gave birth to their second child on the weekend I'd been admitted to hospital, and the contrast felt stark. My work colleagues sent flowers, as did many friends. Our minister visited us and shared Psalm 33—verses which will always remind me of our baby.

Miscarriage is a bereavement. We appreciated those who "mourn with those who mourn." God provided us with comfort and support from our church, family, and friends. The joy of our child's existence was overshadowed by the sadness that death had occurred far too soon from our perspective. But explaining hope and my conviction of God's goodness through tears was powerful, especially to those who were unfamiliar with trusting Jesus.

For us, miscarriage became one part of a long journey of infertility, which included several more years of raw grief and painful decision-making. I cried in church weekly over these years. It is both comforting and confronting to sing of God's absolute control, perfect plans and faithfulness. Only the promises in the Bible could soothe my aches as, over time, it became devastatingly clear that we were unlikely ever to have birth children.

As I read the Gospels, the compassion and perfect solace of Jesus walked off the page to comfort and sustain me. It was tempting to covet friends' situations of pregnancy and parenthood. But I regularly reminded myself that God decides our situation. He wisely and lovingly determines the future.

I never became pregnant again. Eight years after we first began hoping that we'd become parents, we welcomed a son and daughter through adoption. We had been growing increasingly aware of how many children are in desperate need of belonging to a family, so adoption did not feel like Plan B. In fact, earthly adoption is a shadow that points to the wonderful reality that we ourselves become God's children through adoption.

The arrival of any new baby was a time for celebration in our church community. I treasure the memory of the crisp autumn morning when we arrived at a monthly breakfast gathering, bringing our toddler son and baby daughter to meet their church family for the first time. We were greeted with excitement and tears from friends who had supported us over many years. As we fumbled with an array of bibs, comfort toys, dummies, pram and baby bag, I joked that we hadn't arrived late due to sleeping in! While we were happily absorbed by the intensity of becoming parents to two small children, the community around us was overwhelmed with delight just at meeting them. That happiness was a small taste of the profound joy of being adopted into God's family.

# Tethering Yourself to God's People

Days after our baby's body left mine, I pressed random icons in a text message type line until the little pregnant-lady emoji disappeared from my "recently used" keyboard. I deleted the app that tracked development. I "muted" a few friends on social media to avoid seeing photos of their growing bellies or newborn babies. I tried to limit factors that would exacerbate the pain. Unfortunately, a lot of those factors were in my church.

Pregnant women, families, baby dedications and baptisms, prayers for mothers: church services are filled with sights and words that can trigger or magnify the sadness of a bereaved mother. It's tempting to stay away.

So what do we do with Hebrews 10 v 24-25?

> *Let us consider how to stir up one another to love and good works, not neglecting to meet together, as is the habit of some, but encouraging one another, and all the more as you see the Day drawing near.*

The word translated "meet together" describes the formal gathering of believers for corporate worship. Church is meant to be something that God's people orient their lives around.

I once heard a sermon from pastor and teacher Alistair Begg on this passage in which he said, "To be necessarily absent is one thing, but to be needlessly absent is to deprive oneself of being helped and helping others." When we are feeling reluctant or unable to go to church, these words remind us that David's prayer in Psalm 139 v 23-24 is one that we desperately need to pray ourselves. Isolating ourselves needlessly is a "grievous way." But we need the Holy Spirit to search our hearts and help us to discern the difference between what is necessary and what is needless.

*Necessary* might mean that you are sick. You might need to stay home because you are still bleeding heavily, are severely anemic or weak, or are recovering from an operation. But pain is not always physical; perhaps you are not able to attend because you cannot sit in church without having a panic attack or hyperventilating from heaving sobs.

The line becomes fuzzy when we cross from *unable* to *uncomfortable*. This takes discernment. It may seem as if going to a church meeting right now is the last thing you need, and it may be a few weeks before you truly are *able* to attend, but if that is where you are right now, keep considering Alistair's words: "to be needlessly absent is to deprive oneself of being helped and helping others."

First, how might not attending church deprive you of being helped?

Corporate worship is endlessly valuable. Through teaching, communion, corporate confession, and songs, we are reminded of the faithfulness of our Father, who knows the sorrow of losing a child; the sympathy and intercession of our Savior, whose body was broken for us; and the comfort of the Spirit, who is present in and among us. As we look up and around, we are also protected from believing we are alone. And when we join in singing with other saints, or let tears flow as we simply listen to their voices, we are prompted to praise God and to remember the truth of the gospel. Sometimes those voices carry our weary, doubting hearts, declaring over us the words we desperately need to hear and are struggling to sing—or believe—ourselves.

Our church is meant to be a context in which we experience love and care. Sadly, this is not always the case. I recently shared with a counselor friend of mine that I probably didn't attend a church service without crying for at least nine months after our loss. "I'm grateful to hear that," she replied. "It must mean that your church is a place where it is safe for people to weep." This had not always been her experience.

My sister, if your church doesn't feel like a safe place in which to cry, to hurt, or to lament, I am so deeply sorry. But in light of this sad reality, I want to gently ask you to consider, secondly, how you might be a help to your church.

The writer of Hebrews calls his readers to consider how they might stir one another up to love and good deeds. People in pain are able to help others in their church to understand godly grief, to see that it is possible to walk through trials while clinging to Christ, and to grow in expressing lament together. Without the presence of hurting people in the body of Christ, a church is unable to weep with those who weep. I am so grateful that my friend Christi continued to join with our church when she was balding from chemotherapy, even though the rest of us had hair. I'm so thankful that my friend Jayna continues to come to church as a single mom, even though many of us walk in with our children in the arms of our husbands. The church needs its suffering members. Your church needs you.

You don't have to volunteer in the nursery or intentionally approach every pregnant woman you see. Remaining tethered to God's people might look like dipping your toe in: sneaking in a little late and leaving a little early at first. It may look like asking someone you trust to stand beside you. It might mean preparing short responses to "How are you doing?" or growing in the art of asking questions and listening to others. It might even mean meeting privately with your pastor or an elder as a first step in helping your church to understand how they can better love their hurting members.

However it may look, just remain tethered to God's people. Approach slowly and with caution if you must— but don't cut the rope.

**READ:** Romans 12 v 13-17; 1 Corinthians 12 v 12-26

**REFLECT:** What feels scary or intimidating about meeting with your church in the wake of your loss? List these things in detail.

Prepare a few responses to the question "How are you doing?" Think in advance about how much you would want to share in different scenarios, and how you might steer the conversation away from yourself.

**RESPOND:** Ask God to search your heart and reveal the difference between staying away from your church when it is necessary and when it is needless. Ask him to give you the grace and the courage, when it *is* time and you *are* able, to show up, be helped, and help others.

 **JOURNAL**

# Rejoicing With Those Who Rejoice

In the twelfth chapter of Romans, the apostle Paul offers a list of instructions concerning how the church ought to relate to one another. In verse 15 he writes, "Rejoice with those who rejoice." This seems like a no-brainer at first glance. "Congratulations!" and "I'm so happy for you" are phrases we know to say when someone graduates or gets married or finishes a big project. But rejoicing with others becomes difficult when the thing they are rejoicing over is something that we desire.

It is not wrong to desire a biological child nor to grieve the loss of one. It is not wrong to see the round belly of another woman and feel sad because it reminds you of what you have lost, or to watch a mother kiss the head of her newborn and grieve over a future without your own child.

But we cross from godly grief into the "grievous way" of covetousness when we desire what someone else has more than we desire God himself or the good of our neighbor. We make an idol of our desires when we believe they could do what only God can: "If only I had a baby, then I would be happy/fulfilled/at peace." "If only I was still pregnant, then I wouldn't struggle with these negative feelings toward her."

The cure for covetousness is not obtaining what we desire. Even if you were to receive another child, covetousness would pop up somewhere else, because it isn't an issue of circumstances; it's a matter of the heart. Perhaps you would desire an easier pregnancy, a healthier baby, or a child that slept better and cried less. Perhaps it would be something completely unrelated. But there would be something. For the envious heart, there always is.

Thankfully, however, there *is* a cure for covetousness and a key to contentment. We need to remember God's control and his character.

Psalm 139 makes it clear that the circumstances of your life, as well as the circumstances of the woman who has what you long for, are ordained by God. The days of your baby and your neighbor's baby were both numbered by the Creator and Sustainer of life independently of one another. Your neighbor is not responsible for the loss of your baby nor the life of her own.

Recognizing God's control without remembering his character might lead us to believe that he is cruel for withholding something from us. But God does not rule apart from his perfect wisdom and love. Paul writes in Romans 8 v 32, "He who did not spare his own Son but gave him up for us all, how will he not also with him graciously give us all things?"

When we see that God did not withhold his own Son, we can believe that anything he does withhold, he withholds in love. This restores our ability to be content in all circumstances and to love our neighbor as the Bible commands, because we know that his plans for his children are perfectly wise and perfectly loving. We can also see the creation and sustaining of any and all life in a world marked by sin and death as something to rejoice over: a sign of his goodness and his redemptive purposes.

Seeing life through the lens of God's character and control moves our hearts from covetousness to compassion. Rather than seeing our neighbor as an enemy simply because she possesses that which we desire, we become able to rejoice with her even as we weep.

In that same verse, Romans 12 v 15, Paul also tells us to "weep with those who weep." That, too, can be a challenge when the woman who has what we want is lamenting because of the very thing we desire: when she complains about nausea or heartburn from a difficult pregnancy, when she cries from the exhaustion of being up with a night-waking child, or when she expresses her frustration over a trying stage with her two-year-old. If she is in possession of the thing we believe would make us happy, then we cannot see how she should be permitted to feel anything but happiness.

But when we know that the pregnancy or the possession of children is not the cure for trouble, we become able to say, "That must be hard—I'm so sorry," without dismissing her as ungrateful or petty. Or perhaps, rather than curtly responding (aloud or in our minds), "I'd give anything to have that struggle instead of a dead baby," we can gently let her know in love, "I can imagine that must be so hard, but it is also really hard for me to hear you complain about the thing I'm longing for."

Those words might feel impossible to say right now. Perhaps you don't feel it would be possible to even open your mouth without bursting into tears or betraying angry thoughts. But if you feel defeated and helpless when you think about the idea of rejoicing with your neighbor, you're in an ideal posture for prayer. We cannot squelch covetousness or conjure up empathetic feelings on our own. We need the Holy Spirit to help us.

David's final words in Psalm 139 remind us that we need God's help to distinguish between triggered sadness and sinful covetousness. They also remind us that we need him to empower us to obey his commands to love him and to love our neighbor. It's ok to skip the baby shower. It might even be necessary to mute the social-media posts. But grief doesn't give any of us license to hate the woman who has what we long for. Thankfully we have a sympathetic high priest who is faithful to convict, ready to forgive, and willing and able to help. He can restore your faith in his character and control, and he can help you to rejoice and weep with your neighbor, even as you continue to grieve and to heal.

**READ:** 1 Peter 2 v 1-3; Matthew 22 v 36-40

**REFLECT:** Have you struggled at all to rejoice with someone else? How have you felt recently when listening to women complaining about motherhood or children?

What do those reactions reveal about the place of your desire in relation to your worship of God? How can you discern the difference between triggered sadness and sinful covetousness?

**RESPOND:** *Search me, God, and know my heart. Please reveal where I am envious and lead me in the way everlasting: loving, worshiping, and trusting you above all else, and loving my neighbor as myself.*

 **JOURNAL**

# Grace for Your Fumbling Neighbor

*"What were some of the painful things people said in response to your miscarriage?"*

After I put out this question on social media, my eyes welled up with tears as I read through hundreds of responses in disbelief.

*"I don't understand why you're making such a big deal out of this."*

*"Your older child is still a baby. This is probably for the best."*

*"There will be other babies. One day you won't remember or miss this one."*

*"At least you weren't very far along."*

*"Is it even really a considered a baby at this point?"*

*"God must have known you weren't ready to be parents."*

*"At least you know you can get pregnant."*

*"Better it didn't survive. This is just your body's way of getting rid of a defective baby."*

Reading varying forms of those eight replies, I felt angry that people had responded to bereaved mothers of unborn children with so little care, such meager knowledge, and a failure to empathize. I felt angry that the grief of these women was compounded by those unfeeling and uninformed responses.

I can remember people making similar comments to me after my own miscarriage. Or doing things that hurt me. I had never felt the urge to lash out that way before. I found myself clenching my fists at complete strangers or thinking of sharp or biting responses that sometimes escaped from my lips. I wanted to punish the one uttering these painful platitudes or performing these hurtful acts. I wanted to hurt them in the way that they had hurt me.

A few devotions back, we were reminded of the undeserved mercy and grace that we have been shown in Christ Jesus. Because we have been shown great mercy, we are called to be merciful toward those who hurt us. Paul writes to the church at Ephesus, "Be kind to one another, tenderhearted, forgiving one another, as God in Christ forgave you" (Ephesians 4 v 32). We are not instructed to forgive someone because they meant well, or because they don't know any better. If we forgive as Christ has forgiven us, then forgiving our neighbors should have nothing to do with their merit. Whether we imagine that the person who hurts us is well-meaning or not, and whether they speak from ignorance or overdraw from their own experience, we are to show them mercy because we have been shown mercy in Christ Jesus.

Paul also instructs us to be "tenderhearted." A tender heart is forgiving and merciful. But forgiveness and mercy are not things we can produce within ourselves. Thankfully, Jesus doesn't just set the standard for us; he empowers us to obey his commands. And so we must pray with David, for God to search our hearts, to try and test our thoughts, to reveal where we are unmerciful, and to transform our judgmental and calloused hearts into hearts that are tender and forgiving. Instead of continuing on our own shortsighted vengeful way, we need the Holy Spirit to lead us in his everlasting way. He alone can enable us to extend grace even in our pain to those whose questions, comments, and actions are offensive and painful.

Exercising forgiveness and responding with grace doesn't mean we have to pretend the words of others don't hurt. Forgiving someone doesn't mean leaving an offense unaddressed. We can respond with grace but also with truth—helping to correct false or painful comments. Rather than responding from a vengeful place with the goal of putting people in their place, we can engage with them in love, longing to help them understand and to protect them from unknowingly hurting others. We can obey Paul's call to "be kind to one another." Consider these responses:

"Oh, don't you think it's time for a little brother or sister?"

*"We are trying to trust the Lord's timing. Will you pray for us to be patient?"*

"Well, at least you weren't very far along."

*"I know. But even this early, the loss of a baby is still sad and traumatic. I am grieving the child we won't get to hold."*

"You can just try again."

*"It may be some time before we feel ready. But no baby will ever replace the child we've lost."*

"Maybe God knew you weren't ready to be parents."

*"My heart longs for an explanation, but that one is painful to imagine. Would you be willing to simply be sad with us rather than trying to make sense of it?"*

I remember once when I was a girl, my mother and sisters and I came upon a wounded horse on the road. It had been hit by a car and was badly injured. My mom called professionals and we waited for them to arrive, but when my sister begged to get out and comfort the horse, Mom refused. She told us that wounded animals often lash out in their pain and confusion, even at those who are trying to help.

So often, grieving people are the same. We need to be receiving the comfort and care of God so that our pain will not cause us to explode on other people or think murderous thoughts about them in our hearts. We must be grounded in his grace so that we can be gracious with others when they fumble and their words land on raw places. Making our hearts soft, tender, forgiving, and kind is a work that only our Father can do. Ask him to do it for you.

**READ:** Matthew 18 v 21-35; Ephesians 4 v 29-32

**REFLECT:** What painful things have people said or done to you upon learning that you have miscarried? How have you typically responded?

Imagine that you are the servant who has been forgiven much in Matthew 18 and that the person saying something insensitive is the man outside the gate. Does thinking this way change your perspective?

**RESPOND:** Confess to God the ways in which you have been unmerciful or unkind in your response to the comments of others in the wake of your miscarriage. Ask God to create in you a tender heart, quick to forgive when that is undeserved, even as Christ has forgiven you.

 **JOURNAL**

LORE FERGUSON WILBERT

# Enough

We had been married four months when I began to bleed, profusely and painfully: our first miscarriage. I was optimistic. This was my first pregnancy; one in four pregnancies ends in miscarriage. I knew the statistics, and I was just one of them. I didn't weep at all.

Soon, we were expecting a baby again, and beginning to dream of names and baby toes and fingers. I was standing at the back of my church when I felt a sharp and shooting pain nearly buckling my knees, and a rush of blood again. This one was faster, furious, and painful. I sobbed for hours in my husband's arms at home. I felt like a shell of the person I had been only a year before—a joyful, expectant, "about to be married and start her dream job" woman. I *was* a shell of that person.

I felt like a walking tomb: my only purpose to house death. My doctor ran some blood tests and said that the miscarriages were probably due to stress and I should get counseling. I sleepwalked through the year, bearing the miscarriages as they came again and again, unsure of how to de-stress myself enough to the point where my body could carry a baby to term, or even past the first month. For months, I ached.

At some point, the cloud parted. Nate's Bible, an NASB, translates Psalm 73 v 28 like this: "The nearness of God is my good." And God began to show me that he hadn't left at all, and nothing I could do could put me more in his way if I tried. No matter how much of a walking tomb I felt, or how far from God I felt, he was still drawing near to me. He was near me, and this reality was my only good.

I had been single for 34 years and spent most of them desiring marriage. I knew a simple desire for a thing didn't guarantee the getting of it. Now it occurred to me that the same thing was true of children, and, just as singleness had been a gift to me in its time, ordained by God for my good and his glory, childlessness could be too. This subtle shift in my soul began to change everything. The nearness of children or the promise of them were not my good. The nearness of God was my only good, and I was learning that however his nearness comes—in silence, in greatness, in provision, in lack, in fullness, or in meagerness—it is enough.

There is a traditional song sung at the Jewish celebration of Passover. Its name is "Dayenu," which means "It would have been enough." There are fifteen stanzas, each one building on the work of God on behalf of his people through the Old Testament:

> *If he had only brought us out of Egypt, it would have been sufficient. If he had split the sea,*

*it would have been enough. If he had given the*
*Torah, it would have been sufficient.*

On and on it goes, but because those who are reciting the stanzas miss the reality—that the story of captivity, release, provision, and the creation of the temple is one grand illustration of the gospel—the song ends there for them.

Yet we who are in Christ could add verse after verse after verse for all eternity, knowing true "Dayenu" through the life, death, and resurrection of Christ; if God had only done this one thing, it would have been sufficient. One time and for all, his death was and is and always will be sufficient. This portion that we have in Christ, with children or without them, is sufficient. Christ is enough.

Psalm 73 continues, "Whom have I in heaven *but you*? And there is nothing on earth that I desire besides *you*. My *flesh and my heart* may fail, but God is the strength of my heart and my *portion* forever" (v 25-26, emphasis mine).

This belief carried me. He was sufficient. He was my portion. Nothing on earth would satisfy like him.

The miscarriages stopped for a time, or if they came, they were so early that they were mostly undetectable. We determined to give our finances and time and energy to hospitality: to filling the corners of our home—if not with our own children, then with God's children.

Then four years later, one mid-June morning I was leaning over our vegetable garden, and I felt a twinge in my abdomen unlike any I'd felt before. I didn't think I was pregnant, but I began spotting and thought, *Here we go again.*

I waited a week and nothing changed. *Maybe,* I thought, *I am pregnant, and this is what it's supposed to feel like. Maybe this is good.*

One evening, two weeks later, as we got ready for bed, I doubled over in pain. It was so intense that I couldn't breathe.

In the ER, they put me in a bed, ran an IV, put me on morphine, and drew blood. Somewhere in the fog of it all, the doctor came in. I was indeed pregnant, he told me. And then…

"We can't be sure until we run more tests, but I suspect your pregnancy is…"

"Ectopic?" I interrupted him.

"Yes," he said, his eyes flickering down.

My baby was unviable, and if left alone, the doctor said, my reproductive system would rupture, and I would almost certainly die.

We decided not to follow the medical advice to terminate, but to stay in the hospital on close watch. We prayed, knowing that we didn't have to—and needed not to—put our trust in getting the thing we wanted.

We settled in to wait for my body to miscarry naturally or for the baby to miraculously move or for the doctors to tell us that surgery was non-negotiable. We postured our hearts in submission to God, begging for the impossible but trusting him with the probable.

A week later, my blood pressure was dropping, the pain

wasn't abating, and the risk was too high. They surgically removed my ruptured fallopian tube and the dead baby.

Grief is a strange thing, yet I am no stranger to it. And in some ways my grief brought something of a gift with it. *Dayenu, daughter,* the Lord reminded me. *Is this answer sufficient? Even if it's not the one you wanted? Am I enough?* And somehow, he was and it was. Maybe for the first time.

For whatever reason, my body is too high-risk for a baby. We could go through thousands of dollars and dozens of tests and multiple attempts to gain what God has not given us, and we still could end up unable to have children. Or we could trust that God builds families in different ways, through different means; and sometimes those means are fostering or adoption. Or sometimes simply childlessness.

We are trusting that our inability to have children is God's blessing. It's not emptiness to him. It's not wasted. Sometimes God says to a man and a woman, *This is sufficient. Together, the two of you, because I am near you and Christ has come, this is enough. This is good and enough.* Not second-best, not runner-up, not settled-for, not "We'll take what we can get." This is sufficient because God is in it, and he is near, and every promise in him is yes and amen, good and enough. Good enough.

# More than Motherhood

*"Q: What is the chief end of man?*
*A: To glorify God and enjoy him forever."*

This is the first question in the Westminster Shorter Catechism. As a child I was peppered with the question, "What do you want to be when you grow up?" I wanted to be a mom. I wanted that so much that anytime anyone would mention anything about Christ's return, I would think, "But I don't want him to come back before I have a baby!" I truly believed that this was my "chief end" or greatest purpose. There's probably a good reason for that. Growing up, I heard it said over and over that being a wife and a mother is a woman's highest calling. But the first question of this seventeenth-century question-and-answer summary of Christian truth exposes that damaging line of thinking as a lie.

When our desire to have a child, or to have another child, becomes greater than our desire for God himself, our souls shrivel. Rather than feeling secure, peaceful, and prepared, we will be discontented, fearful, and selfish.

This is the effect of worshiping anything instead of God. An idol doesn't have to be a carved image or a golden calf; even a good thing is an idol if it takes God's place in our hearts. Idolatry is a "grievous way": a way that leads to grief—a way that leads to death. But the worship, glory, and enjoyment of God is a way "everlasting"—a way that leads to life.

If our sense of purpose lies solely in motherhood, the loss of an unborn baby can lead to a feeling of worth-lessness. But if we believe that our chief end or highest calling is "to glorify God and enjoy him forever," then we can be filled with purpose and satisfaction in any season and any role.

In Ephesians 2 v 10, Paul writes, "For we are [God's] workmanship, created in Christ Jesus for good works, which God prepared beforehand, that we should walk in them." These works might not be the works we would have chosen for ourselves. He may or may not have planned the good work of motherhood or the good work of mothering multiple children for you. But you can glorify God by walking in the works he has prepared today, actively looking for them as you surrender your desires with open hands to the hands that fashioned you.

Proverbs 16 v 9 reminds us, "The heart of man plans his way, but the LORD establishes his steps." In our quest for meaning, most of us create an ideal of what our lives should look like: a particular career, an age by which we'll be married, how long we'll wait before starting a family, how many children we'll have, how far apart they will be in age, and so on. But though we may make our plans, we do not determine our path. And when the steps God establishes for us look different than the way we had planned for ourselves, we must remember that the Lord's plans are made with perfect wisdom and complete loving kindness.

When we believe that fulfillment is found in motherhood (and in a particular picture of motherhood that we've painted for ourselves), life begins to feel meaningless if we don't have a child or more than one child or children close together. Yet we were never meant to derive significance from a created thing, but rather from the Creator himself.

The highest calling of a woman is not to have children. The greatest purpose of your life is not to be a mother. It is to bring glory to God and to enjoy him. Being a woman of God does not depend upon your marital status or the fruit of your womb but upon the condition of your heart.

Have you found yourself believing that if you could just be a mother—if you could just have a successful pregnancy—or if you could just have another child, then you would be happy and fulfilled? My friend, while I ache with you in your longing, I must tell you, no earthly role or relationship can ever bring you the fulfillment you desire, because you were designed for the glory and enjoyment of God. Right worship puts good desires in their proper place: with God on the throne of your heart, you move from believing that "If I could just get ____, then I would be fulfilled," to being able to say,

"Even if I never get ____, I will still be satisfied because I have Jesus." If the Holy Spirit reveals that motherhood or having another child is an idol for you, ask him to "lead [you] in the way everlasting," as David does. Only the Spirit can change your heart and rightly order your desires and affections.

Contrary to the anxiety I felt as a child that Christ might return before I got to realize my fill-in-the-blank answer on the kindergarten worksheet, I now believe that knowing and treasuring Christ is better than any earthly thing. It's taken loss to show me that. All of our other earthly roles will end, but the purpose of our existence will remain the same throughout all eternity. This is "the way everlasting." The best part of heaven won't be the absence of anxiety, sin, or death but the fullness of the presence of God—and what will be our greatest joy then should be our greatest joy now.

Whether you are able to conceive and have another child, and whether you become a mother through carrying a baby to term or adoption, or you never do, the way everlasting is not a way that will disappoint. Even if you aren't walking into the good works you *wish* he had prepared for you, God is still able to use you. Beyond any role or relationship, he is the One who gives you eternal purpose and significance and joy.

**READ:** 1 Corinthians 10 v 31; Psalm 73 v 24-26

**REFLECT:** Has the desire to be a mother, to be pregnant, or to have another child made it difficult to feel a sense of purpose or worth in your current season?

What do you think it might look like for you to glorify God and enjoy him today?

**RESPOND:** Pray with David that God would lead you "in the way everlasting:" that he would reveal to you the good works he has prepared for you to walk in, and that he would help you to glorify him and enjoy him as you do them, loving him most.

 **JOURNAL**

# Moving Forward

The baby didn't appear to have grown since our initial visit. The ultrasound tech left the room to get our doctor, and I hoped. Hoped that her measurements were off. Hoped that she was incompetent. Hoped that the baby was tucked in a corner. Hoped that my doctor would walk in and discover the flicker that the tech had missed. I didn't brace myself for the blow that might be coming: I simply hoped. But the doctor walked in and looked briefly at the screen, and then at me. "I'm just so sorry."

With a strange matter-of-fact gentleness, he informed me that our baby's little heart had likely given out soon after we initially rejoiced to hear its beautiful, hoof-beat-like sound. I felt foolish for the heaving sobs of shock that poured forth as my mind grasped the meaning of his words.

How could I not have known? I felt so out of touch with my body—with my child. If their assumptions based on measurements were true, our baby's tiny form was already lifeless when we shared the news of our pregnancy with family and friends less than two weeks earlier. I had invited others into the joy and hopeful expectation of a life growing within me when my uterus was already a tomb.

The disappointment of miscarriage can give birth to a hardness of heart. In attempts to guard against facing the shock of trauma or feeling duped again, we arm ourselves with cynicism, beating down thoughts of the future with sticks of fatalistic thinking, refusing to allow ourselves to hope.

The apostle Paul's words in Romans 5 are sweet to those of us who are afraid to hope as a result of the shame we've felt in the wake of disappointment. He speaks of a sure and certain hope that "does not put us to shame" (v 5).

The solution to bearing the ache of disappointment as we walk into an unknown future is not to give up hope but to redirect it.

Suffering loss gives us the beautiful gift of identifying the need for this reorientation. It beckons us to discover the secret of contentment in all circumstances as it invites us to remove our hope from uncertain earthly outcomes and instead to anchor it firmly in certain spiritual realities.

God does not require that we put our desires to death. Fatalism and hopelessness have no place in the heart of a person with a worldview shaped by God's word; we know that God is "making all things new" and is "able to do far more abundantly than all that we ask or think" (Revelation 21 v 5; Ephesians 3 v 20). But our longings becoming realities cannot be our ultimate hope.

That must rest in the character and promises of God, which never disappoint.

And the character and promises of God are just what we have spent the past 30 devotions exploring. As you read and remember, pause to drink in each truth, and pause to praise him as his Spirit prompts you.

He is *all-seeing,* watching over every detail of our lives and looking after us with perfect care and wisdom. He is *all-knowing,* acquainted with our sorrow not just by omniscience but also by experience in the person of Christ, knowing our every thought and giving our finite minds the ability to rest when faced with mystery. He is *everywhere present,* hemming us in where we are weak, walking with us in pain and suffering, comforting us by his Spirit, helping us when we feel overwhelmed, hearing us when we pray, and upholding us when our faith goes out of view.

He is *all-powerful,* knitting life together in the womb, creating us and our babies fearfully and wonderfully, working everything out for the good of those who love him, determining the length of our lives in perfect love and wisdom, using our pain to help us to care for others, governing all of history for the sake of his glory and the good of those who love him, and ultimately defeating all evil.

He is *completely good, loving, and trustworthy,* revealing himself through his word, by which he assures us that he is *faithful* to do all that he promises. He promises to bring the work he has begun to completion. He is at work within us, changing our hearts, making us more like Jesus, rooting us more deeply in the reality of who he is, and making us people of joy. We can have certain confidence that God is using our circumstances to produce endurance and character, growing our hope in the coming glory.

Even in the wake of broken dreams and very real loss, all of God's *promises* are still "Yes" and "Amen" in Jesus (2 Corinthians 1 v 20). They are as good as fulfilled. Because Christ was raised, we can have every confidence in our own future bodily resurrection. It is a coming reality, not a wishful dream.

As we walk forward into a future that is unknown to us, we can embrace with certainty the comfort that comes from the knowledge of who God is, the fact that he is with us, and the assurance that he is leading us by his grace toward a new heaven and a new earth, where there will be no more sorrow, no more pain, and no more babies that die too young (Isaiah 65 v 19-20). Regardless of whether or not she is ever able to carry any future babies to term, this is the sure, fixed, and certain future of the woman who places her hope in Jesus. It will bring greater satisfaction and joy than the realization of any earthly hope.

So, sister, place your hopes in God's character and promises, for that is a hope for which you will not ultimately be made to feel foolish. Hope in the current and coming glory of God without fear or shame, because in the death and resurrection of Jesus, you and I find the absolute certainty that God's plan of redemption can never be miscarried.

**READ:** Hebrews 6 v 16-20; Isaiah 65 v 17-25

**REFLECT:** Did you experience shame or a sense of foolishness for feeling hopeful for the baby that you miscarried? Have you been tempted toward cynicism as a form of self-protection?

Which aspects of God's character or promises bring you the most hope as you move forward after loss?

**RESPOND:** Share with God the earthly hopes and fears you have as you move forward into the unknown. Ask him to help you to hold fast—by his own power and might—to who he is, what he has done for you, and all that he has promised.

 **JOURNAL**

# About the Contributors

**ABBEY WEDGEWORTH** is a wife, mother, and writer. She is passionate about discipleship and Bible literacy, and loves to see the way that the gospel transforms how people think and live. She lives on the South Carolina coast with her husband, David, and their two young sons.

**ISOBEL BURDEN** lives in Cambridge, UK. She is a primary-school teacher but loves most to teach children about the God who made and loves them.

**ERIC SCHUMACHER** is a songwriter and pastor in Ames, Iowa. He is co-author of *Worthy: Celebrating the Value of Women* and serves on the Board of Directors for Risen Motherhood.

**IRENE SUN** was born in Malaysia and lives in the US. She is currently waiting upon the Lord with her preacher husband, Hans, while they raise their four sons. She is the author of the picture book *God Counts: Numbers in His Word and His World.*

**LAUREN WASHER** lives with her husband and children in Virginia. She blogs at www.laurenwasher.com about the things God teaches her about himself, his word, and the life of faith.

**KRISTIE ANYABWILE** is a writer, speaker, mother, and pastor's wife in Southeast Washington, DC. She enjoys spending time with family, cooking, and discipling women.

**JESSALYN HUTTO** serves alongside her husband in his ministry as a church planter near Houston, Texas. She blogs at www.jhutto.com and is the author of *Inheritance of Tears: Trusting the Lord of Life When Death Visits the Womb*.

**COURTNEY REISSIG** is a wife, mother, writer, and speaker. She is the author of *Teach Me to Feel* and *Glory in the Ordinary*. She lives in Little Rock, Arkansas.

**RUTH HATFIELD** works in Sydney as a paediatric speech and language therapist and volunteers in teaching the Bible in school. With her family she loves being part of a local church.

**LORE FERGUSON WILBERT** has lived all over the US but will always be most at home in the northeast. She writes at www.sayable.net and is the author of *Handle with Care: How Jesus Redeems the Power of Touch in Life and Ministry*.

# Recommended Reading

The chapters in this book were intentionally limited in length, in consideration of your capacity during a fragile season. But in case you would like to read more, here is a list of biblical books and articles from authors I trust. I pray they will minister to you as you walk forward in faith.

## ON MISCARRIAGE
*Inheritance of Tears,* Jessalyn Hutto

## ON SUFFERING
*Walking With God Through Pain and Suffering,* Tim Keller
*Embodied Hope,* Kelly Kapic
*A Place of Healing,* Joni Eareckson Tada
*The Promise Is His Presence,* Glenna Marshall
*Hope When It Hurts,* Kristen Wetherell and Sarah Walton
*Joy in the Sorrow,* Matt Chandler and friends

## ON JUSTICE AND REDEMPTION
*Far as the Curse Is Found,* Michael D. Williams

## ON THE SOVEREIGNTY OF GOD
*Trusting God,* Jerry Bridges

**ON ENVY**
*The Envy of Eve,* Melissa Kruger

**ON FEAR**
*Fight Your Fears,* Kristen Wetherell

**ON LAMENT**
*Dark Clouds, Deep Mercy,* Mark Vroegop

**ON PRAYER**
*A Praying Life,* Paul Miller

**ON BECOMING LIKE JESUS**
*You Can Change,* Tim Chester
*How People Change,* Timothy Lane and Paul Tripp

**ON HOW AND WHY TO STUDY THE BIBLE**
*Women of the Word,* Jen Wilkin

**ON CHURCH COMMUNITY**
*Life Together,* Dietrich Bonhoeffer

**ON MARRIAGE**
*The Meaning of Marriage,* Tim Keller
*Together Through the Storms,* Jeff and Sarah Walton

**TO HELP CHILDREN UNDERSTAND GOD'S GOODNESS IN SUFFERING**
*The Moon Is Always Round,* Jonathan Gibson

**ON THE ETERNAL DESTINY OF BABIES**
*www.desiringgod.org/interviews/why-do-you-believe-that-infants-who-die-go-to-heaven*
*www.desiringgod.org/interviews/are-my-septuplets-in-heaven*

# Acknowledgments

My name may be on the cover, but there are a great many people without whom this book would not exist.

David, my patron, thank you for your unwavering support, consistent prayers, service, and encouragement. I am grateful for all that you sacrificed for the creation of this resource.

Dad, thank you for your belief in this project and teaching me by example how to love others well in the wake of loss. Mama, for every way you "showed up" during our loss and the writing of this book, thank you. Erin, thank you for affirming the need for this resource and encouraging me to write it. Jamison, thank you for all that you are to me and have been to this project. Words fail.

Gigi and Marsha, thank you for caring for the boys so I could write, and for your enthusiastic support of this endeavor.

To our family at Hilton Head PCA: you shepherded us through our season of sorrow and supported us through the writing of this book. The summers you devoted to teaching and leading us in singing the psalms, especially those of lament, influenced this work greatly.

Kristen Wetherell, thank you for suggesting that I pursue publication and for the introduction to TGBC. Rebecca and Emily, thank you for your consistent check-ins and exhortation to keep going when I wanted to quit. Thank you to my friends who have shared their losses and experience with me, and to each woman who served this project by reading and offering feedback while her loss was still so fresh. Becky Peters and Hope Blanton, your wisdom as counselors touched me and this book.

Maggie, Lauren, and Caroline, thank you for your consistent encouragement, prayers, and wisdom.

To those who contributed testimonies, I am humbled beyond measure by your willingness to share your stories in these pages.

And thank you to the entire team at The Good Book Company. Katy, your tender heart and sharp mind made this book what it is. Thank you for being an excellent listener, editor, communicator, and advocate. Carl, thank you for seeing the need for this resource and giving me the opportunity to write it, and lending your wisdom, experience, and time to make it better. André, thank you for loving this book and creating a design that is both gentle and hopeful.

And finally, to my faithful Father. Thank you for the love you have shown me in Christ Jesus. To you alone be all glory, honor, and praise.

**thegoodbook**
COMPANY

**BIBLICAL | RELEVANT | ACCESSIBLE**

At The Good Book Company, we are dedicated to helping Christians and local churches grow. We believe that God's growth process always starts with hearing clearly what he has said to us through his timeless word—the Bible.

Ever since we opened our doors in 1991, we have been striving to produce Bible-based resources that bring glory to God. We have grown to become an international provider of user-friendly resources to the Christian community, with believers of all backgrounds and denominations using our books, Bible studies, devotionals, evangelistic resources, and DVD-based courses.

We want to equip ordinary Christians to live for Christ day by day, and churches to grow in their knowledge of God, their love for one another, and the effectiveness of their outreach.

Call us for a discussion of your needs or visit one of our local websites for more information on the resources and services we provide.

Your friends at The Good Book Company

thegoodbook.com | thegoodbook.co.uk
thegoodbook.com.au | thegoodbook.co.nz
thegoodbook.co.in